Dedication

———⌘———

I dedicate this book to Daniela, my dearest wife, whose graceful presence and steadfast support have been my greatest source of inspiration.

This work could not have come to life without your constant light, boundless wisdom, and unfailing love.

I am endlessly grateful for our journey together, which fills my heart with courage and gives me the strength to embrace every step towards happiness by your side.

STEPS TO
HAPPINESS

HAPPINESS

FLORIN ANTONIE

Translation: Daniela Antonie - AI Assisted
Proofreading: Paula Blaj
Copy Editing: Carmel Print
Cover Design: Endi Teodorescu

ISBN: 9798301293634
Imprint: Independently published

Chapters

Foreword

This book is a journey in search of happiness—a journey through the Word of God. Its uniqueness lies in its psychological approach. While many books have been written about happiness from a biblical perspective, the combination of biblical study with psychological research reveals unexpected, surprising, and deeply valuable insights.

Blending the Bible with psychology might seem unusual, perhaps even daunting for some readers, but it is precisely for this reason that I warmly and confidently recommend this book. The author is a profound scholar of Scripture, a faithful expositor of God's Word, and at the same time, an experienced psychologist.

Professor Doctor Iosif Țon

Chapter 1

Steps to Happiness

When we take a closer, more sincere look at our lives, we often realise with surprise how the cost of every fleeting moment of joy that society offers us keeps rising. We may become too reliant on illusions, chasing a version of life that we never truly get to live. Recognising this unfortunate reality is the first step toward breaking free from the prison of our own minds, opening the door to authentic and lasting happiness grounded in truth and meaning.

In this journey, which I have called "Steps Towards Happiness," we will discover that the pursuit of true happiness doesn't require us to search far beyond the horizon, but rather to turn inward. We need to reconnect with our essence—the way God, the Architect of our mind, soul, and body, created us. True happiness lies in our attitude toward the world, toward life, and most importantly, toward Him, the Creator.

I understand that this perspective might seem uncomfortable to a generation that often takes refuge in relativism and the diverse viewpoints that multiculturalism presents. Multiculturalism has given us a multitude of interpretations and paths to happiness, offering formulas for every taste and social standing[1].

Yet, if we are to truly grasp and embrace the kind of happiness that has stood the test of time, unaffected by changing paradigms, we must reintegrate the wisdom of our forebears into our modern culture.

———————• •———————

The ancient manuscript of the Bible, the cornerstone of our society, science, and culture, teaches us that absolute happiness is not a gift or a fleeting moment but the natural conclusion of our daily attitudes and actions.

———————• •———————

"Blessed are the undefiled in the way, who walk in the law of the Lord!" (Psalm 119:1, NKJV)

What makes you happy? Or what can still make you happy in this unstable society? The simplest answer to this question is: to walk in the law of the Lord – meaning to be a just, ethical, moral, and faithful person in everything you do.

You may question this statement and wonder if it all somehow boils down to spirituality in this hyper-developed world,

---

[1] Bauman, Z., *Liquid Modernity*. Cambridge: Polity Press, 2000.

philosophically, scientifically, economically, politically, and psychologically. The surprising answer is yes! Over time, we have gradually distorted our minds by being overexposed to the transient philosophies of the world, which today present certain facets of philosophy or science as ultimate truths that will be considered outdated or eroded, incomplete or unauthentic tomorrow.

To understand all these aspects, we must return together to our origin as created beings and recognise that the happiness the Creator speaks of can only be found in us if we adopt the proper attitude towards the world and life.

In 1938, researchers at Harvard University initiated a study known as the *Harvard Study of Adult Development* to investigate what qualities can provide absolute happiness to man. This longitudinal study analysed participants throughout their lives. By 2016, in the first 75 years of the study, 724 volunteers had been analysed, some of whom were still alive at the study's publication. Participants were consistently interviewed about their preferences, passions, friendships, marriages, and reactions to stress[2].

The study highlighted three fundamental lessons:

1. **Being social and dedicated to others is essential for life**. Loneliness can profoundly affect us. A happy person is devoted to others, not to themselves. People

[2] Waldinger, R. J., & Schulz, M. S., *The Long Reach of Nurturing Family Environments: Links With Midlife Emotion-Regulatory Styles and Late-Life Security in Intimate Relationships*, 2016.

with strong social ties with family, friends, and community lived longer, were healthier, and remained happy throughout their lives.

2. **The quality of relationships matters more than the quantity.** A famous saying goes, "Tell me who your friends are, and I'll tell you who you are!" Conflictual relationships are more harmful than physical wounds. Divorce or death leaves deep wounds in the soul, while quality relationships strengthen us. The Harvard study underscores that healthy relationships are more important than their number for longevity.

3. **Quality relationships protect the brain.** People with healthy relationships and a good environment develop fewer brain problems, maintaining long-term memory and high IQ.

———————● ●———————

Happiness is therefore not found in material goods or social recognition but in authentic relationships and a profound understanding of human and divine nature in how we dedicate ourselves to others.

———————● ●———————

Thousands of years before this Harvard study, we were told that we were created to form a society that functions like an organism. For example, Christianity, the foundation upon which the modern world was built, operates as an organism where each of us has a specific role, and the priority is to strengthen others. The heart pumps blood to all organs, and the brain thinks for the protection of the whole organism, demonstrating how personal happiness is interconnected with the wellbeing of those around us.

These lessons discovered by the *Harvard Study of Adult Development* have challenged the mindset of the modern generation, which seems to value only wealth and fame. Studies indicate that 80% of contemporary adolescents aspire to gain wealth, while 50% aim for fame, simultaneously wishing to maintain their privacy: I want to be famous but left alone![3]

Thus, we observe a distancing from the fundamental values of humanity. Although we are part of an interconnected civilisation, material values tend to suppress personal values, with modern man focusing on the fleetingness of wealth to the detriment of intelligence, wisdom, and love for our neighbour.

When our Saviour Jesus Christ delivered His first significant sermon – the Sermon on the Mount, recorded in the Gospel of Matthew – He gathered His disciples, sat down, and began speaking to them so the other curious ones gathered around could hear. Once we relearn how to be truly happy, those around us will notice the change within us. Since happiness has become a rarity on earth, everyone will want to learn the fantastic recipe to achieving it.

---

[3] Twenge, J. M., & Kasser, T. *Generational Changes in Materialism and Work Centrality, 1976–2007: Associations With Temporal Changes in Societal Insecurity and Materialistic Role Modeling. Personality and Social Psychology Bulletin*, 39(7), pp. 883-897, 2013.

Have you ever seen a swallow? You will most likely answer in the affirmative. How do you know it was a swallow and not a woodpecker or a hoopoe? What do you base this on? The answer is simple: observable details confirm reality.

Similarly, a believer must be recognised by a specific attitude as God's representative on this earth. Do you know what that is? Happiness! Those around you should see happiness in you.

However, there is a difference between momentary *happiness* and the intense joy that comes from inner fulfilment. Many do not realise that contemporary science and philosophy have distorted reality, so happiness has come to be perceived as a short-lived projection anchored in material things: "I'm happy because I bought a new car!" "I'm happy because I bought a new dress!" Or, „I'm happy because I bought a new TV!"

But after you've longed for it, imagine how it would be, unpack it, and see how it looks propped on the furniture; the magic quickly disappears. Suddenly, that television, dress, or car you thought would bring supreme happiness becomes something trivial which does not bring happiness. This happens because the consumer society has taught us to aim incorrectly. Today, when we talk about happiness, we speak of a form that is not synchronised with what God, the Designer and Creator of man, understood by the word *happiness*, calling it joy.

The difference between joy and *happiness* is that joy comes from within, from the feeling of fulfilment.

To understand these aspects and their differences more clearly, let us analyse the biblical concept of "blessed" and how it can be misapplied in our daily lives. We will thus understand how we have sabotaged ourselves by desynchronising our mentality from what God intended for us from the very beginning and how wrongly we have come to place emphasis on life. The concept of „blessed" is usually conditioned by something: *blessed are you if you do this; blessed are you if you are obedient.*

In the Greek language, in which the New Testament was written, the term used is *"Makarios."* This noun is turned into an adjective that would be translated rather as "happy is the one who..." In other words, it is not a condition but a conclusion for something already achieved.

It is practically the difference between the formulations: *blessed are you if you help your neighbours and you are happy because you helped your neighbours.*

In the first example, we deal with a suggestion specific to the mentality of those who see life as a checklist of achievements that must be ticked off. In the second example, we observe the naturalness of one who acts from an ethical and moral instinct, one for which happiness becomes a reward. In the first example, the emphasis is on action, regardless of the motivation behind it – sometimes mechanical and imitated. In the second one, the emphasis is on the attitude that dictates actions, an attitude that is understood and assumed. In other words, motivation dictates how happiness is lived.

Makarios, in the Greek language, describes what is expressed in Hebrew culture by *"Esher,"* which means "to have a joy streaming from relationships with others"—to be happy because you make others happy, to be happy because you see others satisfied.

In ancient Greek culture, "Makarios" also meant blessing. Practically, when someone said to you, "Be blessed!" they were telling you, "Be happy!"

To conclude, make others happy and do not sadden them. God has blessed us, which means He has made us happy, and we owe it to others to obey the Creator's special request: *"Bless and do not curse!" (Romans 12:14, NKJV).*

And yet, if happiness is, in God's vision, a conclusion and not a recommendation, if joy is a commandment and not generated by yourself but by the presence of Divinity in your life, then why have we reached the point where we are today? Why has happiness become situational and conditioned nowadays? Why does our happiness depend on purchasing an object or a specific type of food?

Do you remember Esau and Jacob? Esau, who sold his birthright for a dish (a lentil stew)? *"Look, I am about to die; what is this birthright worth to me?" (Genesis 25:32, NKJV).*

The philosophy of life we currently follow conditions happiness on the immediate desires of the body rather than the mind. Many interpersonal relationships are based solely on

lust and instinct at the expense of relationships built on character, ethics, and morality. In essence, we are sacrificing what
is inherently valuable in us for aspects of life that hold no real
value.

In the biblical view, *happiness* represents the culmination
of each person's life. You are a happy person not because you
followed a specific algorithm aimed exclusively at happiness
but because you chose to diligently implement the true mechanisms for which you were created on a daily basis. You chose
to be an ethical, moral, and faithful person because this represents the normality of human existence: to live beautifully,
without sin, and in harmony with your fellow beings. When
you become the person God intended and created you to be,
you will experience precisely who you were meant to be: a
happy person.

To grasp this concept, we will examine a few valuable elements from Psalm 1, an ancient literary masterpiece that conveys the Divine wisdom presented to the people of Israel when
they were introduced to the mindset of truly happy individuals.
Psalm 1 begins with the words: *"Blessed is the man who..."* If
I had used the phrase *"Fortunate is the man who...,"* as translated into Romanian, it would suggest I was offering a recommendation or pointing to an ideal to pursue. However, let us
draw on everything we have learned to explore the distinction.

"Blessed is the man who walks not in the counsel of the ungodly, nor stands in the path of sinners, nor sits in the seat of the scornful" (Psalm 1:1, NKJV).

Notice the transition and dynamics: **does not walk, does not stand, and does not sit**. Does it not seem that sometimes we follow this pattern when we make mistakes? At first, we only glance. Then curiosity leads us to stop and observe more closely, and ultimately, we get involved.

Returning to the Biblical text, we notice that the author presents us with the perspective of a person who is already happy, not because they pursued happiness at all costs, but because they chose to be ethical and moral. Blessed is the person who *does not go* – has stopped consulting with the ungodly; who no longer sits with the wicked but finds delight in the law of the Lord. *(Psalm 1:2, NKJV)*

It is important to mention that wickedness and sin exist because of desire, and desire is always associated with pleasure. We never desire things that hurt us. For example, have you ever craved a toothache? Certainly not, because by its nature, a person avoids things that cause pain but, unfortunately, they get involved in those that bring benefits, even at the risk of causing pain to others. We all desire things that give us pleasure, and we all long for this pseudo-happiness.

God also speaks about pleasure here, but within the right frame: pleasure is found in the law of the Lord. This person finds such special delight in the law of the Lord that they meditate on it (verse 2). To meditate means to think deeply, to analyse, to understand the reason behind something. A person who meditates day and night is truly passionate. Have you ever had a passion so great that you thought about it even at night?

Someone once said to me, "I want to feel alive! I'm happiest when I put the pedal to the metal." I asked, "How much is that happiness worth to you?" Without hesitation, he replied, „Oh, I'm willing to pay any fines I might get!

Notice from this example that some people quantify happiness incorrectly because they do not frame it the same way God did but do everything for their own momentary pleasure and desire. However, as long as you remain by God's law, *„you will be like a tree planted by the rivers of water"* (Psalm 1:3, NKJV).

How does a tree planted by a river of water differ from one planted in the desert? How do you recognise it? By its flowers? By its leaves? By its appearance? In the same way, a happy person will easily stand out among others. Not through their grimaces or their frowning, but through the peace within their soul. This person bears fruit. A happy person is full of fruit.

And what is the fruit of a happy person, you may ask? My answer may shock many: your happiness will produce the joy and pleasure of others finding peace next to you.

It is important to note that *"the ungodly are not so"* (Psalm 1:4, NKJV). It may be shocking for many, but the Bible divides people into two major categories in this Psalm:

1. Happy people, who have an ethical and moral character, thus reflecting the image of God.

2. Wicked people, who lack ethics and morals.

In the context of our analysis, where we focus on the concept of happiness, it becomes clear that the Bible places the people from the second category, the wicked, among the unhappy. It is possible that these people find a sort of pseudo-pleasure in money, fame, or other similar things, but none of these will last. Everything will only have an ephemeral and superficial worth. Even if they claim to be happy, it will become clear that their happiness does not align with the parameters set by the Creator and will quickly dissipate.

There is a causal chain between goodness and happiness or between sadness and upset. Have you ever heard of something perfectly good creating sadness? Never. Why, then, are people sad? Because something has been broken. Something is no longer in its place. Something has been compromised due to sin, violence, and stress. For instance, we see parents who are sad because their children have gone astray; spouses who are sad because their partners are no longer the same as they were at the altar; and couples who were once happy but are now saddened, because their partners are no longer the way they once were when they joined their destinies.

———————• •———————

Happiness means being a person of goodness, and goodness always reflects on others, not on oneself.

———————• •———————

"The ungodly are... like the chaff which the wind drives away" (Psalm 1:4, NKJV). If you are unhappy, ask yourself if there might be any trace of wickedness within you, no matter how small. Even a small dose of wickedness is poison.

Have you ever seen chaff? Have you walked down the street in autumn when the wind kicks up the dust and you feel it entering your eyes? In moments like these, nothing can make you happy, because of the discomfort and irritation brought on by the dust. Your only thought is to get home and get rid of that which bothers you. So it is with wicked people: like dust in your eyes. They may not see themselves as wicked, but in the eyes of others, they certainly are a constant source of discomfort.

Here's a direct question for you: do you consider yourself a happy person? If not, you might be like dust in other people's eyes. Do you understand the consequences of this? Unhappy people *"shall not stand in the judgment... nor sinners in the congregation of the righteous" (Psalm 1:5, NKJV).*

Being happy means more than just declaring yourself happy. According to God, being happy is a conclusion of the lives of people who have come to know Him, aspects that we will discuss in detail throughout this book, but which I briefly outline here to motivate you to read it to the end. Truly happy people who have inner peace and who have won the battle against stress, depression, or any form of bondage of modern society are those who first understood that it is they who need to change and that they have failed by themselves. They are those who are empathetic and regret their mistakes. They do not remain prisoners of the lamentations of the past but engage actively to correct their errors. They are not just sympathetic to others, but truly empathetic. Happy people are the persons who aim for righteousness with passion and devotion. They are those who have a clean and clear mind. They are those who bring God's peace all around them.

I sincerely hope that at the end of this book, God's smile may grace your lips! May His peace fill your heart and His beauty as Creator be reflected on your face!

Chapter 2

Princes and Paupers

"Blessed are the poor in spirit, for theirs is the kingdom of heaven" (Matthew 5:3, NKJV).

God created man to be happy and fulfilled, but unknowingly, having fallen prey to the guidance of this world's philosophy, man forgot how to rejoice! In this chapter, please join me in exploring how God wants us to rediscover the state for which He created us—not through the world's failing prescriptions, but by rediscovering joy through a correct framing of life.

Let's set off on our journey by reflecting on the first of the Beatitudes, spoken by our Saviour, as stated in Matthew 5:3 (NKJV): *"Blessed are the poor in spirit, for theirs is the kingdom of heaven!"*

In 1881, a book titled *The Prince and the Pauper* was published in Canada. This book, written by Mark Twain, describes the lives of two boys born on the same day, almost identical in appearance: one a prince and the other a pauper. At one point, they exchange roles: the prince ends up living the life of a pauper, while the pauper gets the chance to temporarily taste princely life. It is a complex book that does not just offer a story with a happy ending, but rather presents a person who, through relevant analysis and exposure to reality, understands who they are and what they were created to be.

We have been ordained by God to be His sons and daughters, His princes and princesses in His Kingdom.

On what basis do I make this claim? In Galatians 4:7 (NKJV) it is written: *"Therefore you are no longer a slave, but a son [and, by extension, daughter]."* We have been adopted from this world and have become the sons and daughters of God. It is important to understand how God wants us to view the reality by which we evaluate ourselves, for then we will understand the mechanisms behind rediscovering lost happiness.

Imagine now two lavish halls connected by **seven small antechambers**, placed one after the other. Whether you like it or not, in order to move between the two large halls, you will have to pass through all the seven antechambers that connect them.

The first large chamber is present life, with its ups and downs. It is the current state in which we feel all the social pressure and stress that society conveys to us; a reality where happiness is a permanent illusion, always out of reach.

The second chamber holds the true state of happiness, perfectly tailored and customised for each one of us. Here, we will find a practical mindset by which we can assimilate this happiness into our own lives.

To lay hold of this precious treasure, we will have to exert effort and energy, committing to travel the entire journey between the two chambers without hesitation and without doubt. We cannot skip any of the seven small antechambers. There is no shortcut or secret door, and we will have to patiently go through all seven chambers, regardless of the traps that await us in each of these.

During our journey, we will gradually understand that these chambers and antechambers actually represent the process each of us must assume and go through to relearn **how to be happy**. We will also need to understand that each antechamber is a specific place where we will reshape our character and re-imprint in us the set of attitudes God intended for man from the very beginning.

Walking this path together, we will learn the seven attitudes we need to regain happiness in our own lives.

Let us all step into the **first antechamber**.

On the frontispiece of its door, deeply carved letters read: *"Blessed are the poor in spirit!" (Matthew 5:3, NKJV).* Practically, it is how God greets us and tells us what to expect: The Kingdom of heaven is, first and foremost, for the poor in spirit.

To make a brief analogy, this frontispiece wants to convey that God will never place diamonds in a palm filled with common pebbles gathered from the field. He wants you to rid yourself of the dirty stones you tightly hold so that He can place in your now empty palm His precious stones, along with His extraordinary values.

Have you ever wondered what the difference is between action and attitude? Many believe that God is telling us what to do here. Due to a faulty translation, we have come to emphasise the idea that if we act in a certain way, we will undoubtedly be happy. We have not understood that, in fact, the expression is: *"Blessed are those who..."* In other words, the attitude with which we act becomes the centre of gravity, and happiness follows unconditionally.

I say this because attitudes are a reflection of our values and beliefs, which later result in action. This is where, in my opinion, Christianity has failed, and this is why we no longer know how to be happy: because we rush to act by imitating others, without understanding why we must do what we do. In His discourse, the Saviour taught us how to have the right attitude towards the world and life; not to do things without understanding them or just because we were told so.

It is clearly stated in contemporary psychology that any behaviour is a reaction to an attitude that the individual has, and these attitudes are a projection of the character, values, and beliefs accumulated throughout life[4]. Even if one belief can be shared by several individuals, the attitude towards that belief is always personalised and filtered through one's own life experiences. It is the way we choose to manifest that belief through our behaviour.

Thus, some people who believe in God say that things must be done a certain way. Others, who believe in the same God, claim that things must be done differently. Some come up with more whimsical ideas, while others with more rigid ones, even though all claim the same belief in the same God. We observe here that the way they relate to belief is different. To understand these differences, it is necessary to mention that although values or beliefs are largely constructed from inherited cultural components, the attitudes with which we relate to values or beliefs are eminently learned and moulded[5].

---

[4] Ajzen, I., *The Theory of Planned Behavior. Organizational Behavior and Human Decision Processes*, 50(2), pp. 179-211, 1991.

[5] Haidt, Jonathan. *The Righteous Mind: Why Good People Are Divided by Politics and Religion*. Vintage Books, 2012.

Considering all these details, the question arises: with what attitude should we start our journey in search of happiness? Well, it is written: *"Blessed are the poor in spirit, for theirs is the kingdom of heaven" (Matthew 5:3, NKJV).*

Unfortunately, some people consider that being poor in spirit means being intellectually stagnant or timid. Etymologically, we are dealing with an ancient expression of the Jewish people, later encountered in Greek culture and transmitted to us as well. Being poor in spirit refers, in simple terms, to the recognition of one's own bankruptcy, but not in the sense of being worthless or aimless, but at that level where we understand that without God, we are merely bankrupt individual[6].

The biblical text does not impose poverty on us to be pleasing to God but urges us to understand that, by ourselves, we are nothing. On the other hand, contemporary philosophy tells us that we can become whatever we desire, if only we truly believe in ourselves. It would be so easy if believing were that simple!

Going further and analysing the expression "poor in spirit" in the original language, we notice its profound spiritual significance. A brief semantic analysis is necessary to properly understand this enigmatic expression of the Saviour.

In the Greek language, poverty is described by two terms: *ptochos* and *penichros*. Ptochos means extreme poverty, like that in Mark Twain's masterpiece, *The Prince and the Pauper*. This term does not refer to the fact that you, having three pounds

---

[6] Willard, Dallas. *The Divine Conspiracy: Rediscovering Our Hidden Life in God.* HarperOne, 1998.

in your pocket, are poorer than someone who has four pounds. *Ptochos* means not even having pockets, let alone money to hold in them. *Ptochos* means being in the situation described in the Gospel of Luke, chapter 16, where it speaks of a poor man who lay at the gate of a rich man dressed in purple and fine linen. Every day, this poor man, named Lazarus, full of sores, longed *"to be fed with the crumbs which fell from the rich man's table. Moreover, the dogs came and licked his sores" (Luke 16:21, NKJV)*. In other words, this man had nothing.

On the other hand, *penichros*, the second term, does not necessarily mean being dirt poor but rather having shortcomings. If you ask people about this, especially in our country, they will always tell you they are poor, that they lack certain things. Almost all of them would say they do not have enough. If, for instance, you had an expensive car and had to sell it for a cheaper one, you would say you did so because you could no longer afford it. In contrast, for a poor person characterised by the concept of ptochos, your cheaper car represents an impressive fortune. An example is in the Gospel of Luke, chapter 21, when Jesus sees a widow casting two mites into the treasury and says, *"Truly I say to you that this poor widow has put in more than all; for all these out of their abundance have put in offerings for God, but she out of her poverty put in all the livelihood that she had" (Luke 21: 3-4, NKJV)*. It is not about this woman giving all her wealth. The term used is *penichros*; Jesus saw a widow with shortcomings, who lacked things; not a dirt-poor widow, but one who gave all she had at that moment. *"All she had to live on"* was all she had to buy food for that day. Practically, the widow refrained from her needs and gave it all.

Why is this terminological differentiation important? Because in our context, in the expression *"Blessed are the poor in spirit" (Matthew 5:3, NKJV)*, the term *ptochos* is used. It is about a person so poor in their spirit that they can no longer look up to the heavens, aware of their utter need for divine intervention. I mentioned earlier that this expression means to think of oneself as bankrupt; to consider that you, by your definition as a human, no longer mean anything and that you can be everything only through God. This attitude must be applied so that you do not see it as a temporary shortcoming, but as a total dependence on God. In other words, it means to unconditionally place yourself in God's hands at every moment.

Lazarus, the poor man, could not set conditions for the rich man. He depended on him and hoped to receive at least his crumbs. He had no claims; he could not force anyone and was content with little. This is how a person who takes God at His word should be.

Believe it or not, the first step to unlocking the chest where the philosophy of the world has trapped our happiness is to recognise our total dependence on God.

I will pause for a short moment to remind you of a key aspect I have already mentioned, but which now becomes clearer.

Being poor in spirit does not imply a mechanical recognition, nor a superficial declaration before others, but a motivated recognition before the Creator, which should come not from an imitated action, but from a thoughtful and assumed attitude. This is the crucial difference. This is where many of us fail, and precisely for this reason, we do not step further, to the second antechamber. This happens because we have instinctual behaviours and actions without understanding what we must do, without educating ourselves and adopting an appropriate attitude. Imitative actions do not come from within our being, but from observing the actions of others. If temperament is something you are born with, character is learned. The attitude towards the world and life is learned.

Why is it important to acknowledge our humble state before God? Because only then can we understand what sincere dependence on Him means. In the hand that once held dirty stones gathered from the dirt in the street, He will place His precious stones, His jewels, which will transform us into good and happy people. Etymologically speaking, there is a connection between being good and being happy.

Being poor in spirit means embracing humility, but not in the way it is often misunderstood in today's world. To clarify, the Oxford English Dictionary defines humility as "the quality of having a modest or low view of one's importance." This implies that true humility cannot involve self-congratulation, such as saying, "Look how humble I am!" Instead, it refers to a sincere attitude of modesty and submission directed towards God.

But what does it mean to be a humble person? Should we dress in tattered clothes? Should we always keep our heads bowed? No, for it is written: *"My lips shall greatly rejoice when I sing to You, and my soul, which You have redeemed" (Psalm 71:23, NKJV).* When you address God, you cannot approach Him with false tears, thinking you can impress Him. But humility does not necessarily mean keeping your head down. Humility is not about action, but about attitude. A joyful person can be extremely humble. Humble people are serene, who never sport frowns, and who understand the level they are on. They also know who their Creator is.

Interestingly, we see humility as an enemy because we are too full of ourselves, too proud. We believe we are important and special. It's no wonder our Lord Jesus tells us in Matthew 16:24 (NKJV): *"If anyone desires to come after Me, let him deny himself, and take up his cross, and follow Me".* There is a profound meaning that He, our Creator, emphasises regarding how God's children should live their lives: they should be happy. And everything begins with self-denial.

You cannot deny yourself until you realise how much emphasis you have placed on yourself. You cannot give up your vices until you become aware of them. Until you understand how vicious pornography is for you, you will not give it up; until you understand how much excessive alcohol poisons you, you will not stop drinking; until you understand how much gossip poisons you, you will continue to gossip; until you understand how much envy poisons you, you will continue to envy others; until you understand how much constant criticism poisons you, you will continue to criticise. Therefore, the Lord Jesus, the Creator, has taught us that we cannot be happy until we come to deny ourselves.

But what does it mean to deny myself? It means to understand that there is a Sovereign above me who created me; to understand that I did not come into existence through a cosmic accident or as a result of some miraculous alignment of the planets, but to understand that, in the beginning, God was the One who created things, that He is in control of everything, and that when I understand that I am a bankrupt person by myself, I will realise that I cannot get anywhere without God. Then, the first chain that has closed the door to happiness will be broken. This chain will break when we truly learn what the old expression "to deny ourselves" means and we apply it in our lives to the letter.

Here is a practical example from which we can learn what it means to be truly poor in spirit, as well as what practical details to pay attention to so as not to err. Our Creator has left us with seven letters He Himself wrote. You will find them in the book of Revelation, in chapters 2 and 3. The last one is the one sent to the Church of Laodicea. To this Church, it was said: *"I know your works, that you are neither cold nor hot" (Revelation 3:15, NKJV).*

God knows your deeds, and the conclusion is simple: you are neither bad nor good. You are somewhere in the middle: one foot in, one foot out. You are comfortable because you tell yourself you are fine. If you read the text carefully, you will notice how God highlights why these deeds are ever-changing and why man is often lukewarm: *"neither cold nor hot."* Why?

Well, "because you say," because you declare, because you have a wrong attitude: *"I am rich, have become wealthy, and have need of nothing" (Revelation 3:17a, NKJV).*

This is the attitude of self-sufficiency: "I have everything, I am doing well; it means God has blessed me." Be careful; this is a principle of faulty causality often encountered in contemporary society. We can believe that if fire heats the pot of food and we can eat it relaxed, then fire is always good. If we were to use the same faulty logic, we could erroneously conclude that the fires of hell are also good, since they're also fire. The same type of thinking can lead us to conclusions like: if I am rich, it means God gave me this wealth, as a sign of His blessing me. Thus, we may end up believing that we accumulated wealth due to our righteousness or diligence, and thus, we lack for nothing. In other words, we are happy with what we have and we would even consider ourselves thankful, without realising how superficial our way of thinking is.

But God says: you *"do not know that you are wretched, miserable, poor, blind, and naked" (Revelation 3:17b, NKJV).* All these came about because your attitude is one of self-sufficiency. Self-sufficiency represents the mentality by which a person believes they are at a level built through their own efforts and involvement. In this context, the consumer society and the online environment play a significant role, by constantly promoting values such as self-confidence and self-worth through ubiquitous motivational messages.

The purpose of these messages, found abundantly on the Internet, is to remind individuals of their own abilities and potential, encouraging self-rediscovery. The concepts of self-sufficiency and self-confidence are seen as fundamental to personal success, according to various theories of psychology[7].

Until we discover how bankrupt
we truly are in and of ourselves,
our lives will not truly begin.

Have you heard the expression "buying money"? It's an interesting concept. What does it mean to buy gold? The process of buying and selling involves volunteering. It involves the seller's desire to sell and the buyer's desire to buy. It implies active, not passive, involvement: to give and to receive. It ultimately means understanding the value as well as the purchase and sale price.

God does not want us to be people with automated minds: He did not create us to be automatons or robots, but He wants us to decide today to step into the first antechamber. Maybe you are stressed or anxious at this moment. Maybe the pressure of war, the financial crisis, job loss, lack of a home, or the relationships in your life give you chills. Understand that in whatever situation you find yourself, if you acknowledge your weakness, guilt, failure, and you evaluate yourself according to God's standards, you will come to take the first step towards self-rediscovery. You will then rediscover the person God created in His image and likeness, and you will understand that

---

[7] Dweck, C. S. (2006). *Mindset: The New Psychology of Success.* Random House Incorporated.

your coming into this world was not an accident. God created you to have an impact on society because you entered this world under the sign and light of divine goodness. If things are not going well for you today, it is because the decisions we make are not in line with the will of the sovereign Architect of the entire universe, the Lord Jesus Christ.

In another letter from the book of Revelation, the author also spoke to another Church, named Smyrna, as follows: *"I know your works, tribulation, and poverty (ptochea) but you are rich" (Revelation 2:9, NKJV).*

The people in this congregation had relinquished themselves and came to believe about themselves that they were the most destitute spiritually, but they depended entirely on God. He tells them that they are, in fact, the richest.

———•———•———

Humble people never believe that God owes them anything for their humility. They are simply dependent on Him, and more than that, they are thankful. They are ready to receive everything He gives them, both good and not-so-good.

———•———•———

Being poor in spirit is the first step toward rediscovering your happiness. Being poor in spirit is the first characteristic of the heirs of the Kingdom of God. Being poor in spirit involves voluntary action, as well as the desire and effort to succeed.

Being "poor in spirit" is not a weakness, but a strength that frees us from the chains of self-sufficiency and opens us to a life full of meaning and divine fulfilment. It is an invitation to renounce the burden of worldly expectations and focus on the authentic values and joys that God offers.

As we go through each stage of this inner transformation, we are reminded that happiness is not a distant destination, but a way of living aligned with His will. Understanding that we are created to be heirs of His Kingdom allows us to embrace our role as His sons and daughters, living with gratitude and joy.

May this realisation inspire us to cast off the burden of the self and open our hearts to the blessings He has prepared for us. The path to happiness is within our reach, and the choice is ours—to embrace with courage and faith the journey toward divine fulfilment.

Chapter 3

---❖---

Humility, Pride and Prejudice

"Thus says the High and Lofty One, whose
habitation is eternity and whose name is Holy:
"I dwell in the high and holy place, but also with him
who is of a contrite and humble spirit, to revive the
spirit of the humble, and to encourage the heart of
the contrite." (Isaiah 57:15, NKJV)

We live in times that make it almost impossible for humans to be happy, detached, and relaxed in their lives. We are threatened by war and overwhelmed by crises—be they financial, political, social, or spiritual—so much so that stress gnaws at each of us to a greater or lesser extent.

In this chapter, we will continue our journey in the first antechamber and analyse the traps that prevent a person from acknowledging their self-failure. We will focus on two destructive elements in a person's life: pride and prejudice, and we will explore the antidote that removes them from each of our lives: humility. We will understand what humility truly is, how it manifests itself in a humble person, how to foster this feature in our life, and how to avoid displaying false humility. We will learn how to start from scratch, recognise our mistakes, and eliminate pride and prejudices from our lives.

Generally, people in whom even the smallest seed of pride has sprouted will always consider themselves superior and above dealing with the trivial matters of life. Once it has sprouted in our minds, the seed of pride can transform us and eliminate any tendency for improvement. A person led by pride or prejudice will do everything in their power to block any information that might reveal their mistakes or show them they are guilty.

The year 1813 saw the publication of the novel Pride and Prejudice, written by Jane Austen. The novel follows and develops the portrait of Elizabeth Bennet, the book's protagonist, who gradually understands the repercussions of her hasty judgments. In time, she comes to appreciate the difference between the superficial kindness displayed by most people and the true kindness that, by definition, is an art.

True kindness always springs from a state of profound humility.

A proud person cannot truly be kind. A proud person cannot be devout. Pride will distort their perception of reality correctly because everything will be filtered through the lens of their own wellbeing. Therefore, they will not be able to make an accurate self-assessment and will not accept that they are dependent on someone. Proud people, by their very definition, consider themselves to be the centre of the universe[8].

For this reason, humility has become the feared enemy of the fundamental bricks our contemporary society is built on—a society that wants man to believe that he is everything in himself, that he is self-sufficient and needs nothing else.

Religion practices that have recently taken shape consider that, through appropriate behaviour, a person can receive God's favour as a kind of salvation obtained exclusively through deeds. In other words, if you know how to behave at the right time and place, you will gain God's favour. But if we look carefully at God's character and mindset, we will understand that man, by himself, can gain nothing, no matter how many good deeds he does in this world. Salvation is received as a gift, and when you receive it, you desire to become like God. The impression that man is self-sufficient has been created by society with the express intention of removing the Creator.

In this picture, humility stands diametrically opposed to the foundations on which postmodern religions are built, which believe that, through a specific formula, you can gain the Creator's favour.

---

[8] Lewis, C.S. *Mere Christianity*. HarperOne, 2001.

————————• •————————

The humble state does not refer to a person's outward appearance but to what they bring out of the chest of their values: how they speak, how they relate to others, and how they uplift them.

————————• •————————

A truly humble person will not seek to be raised and placed at the forefront, nor to be placed on a throne. A humble person will seek to uplift others and, if necessary, to be the servant of all. It is true that the humbler you are, the more blessed you are, but the more blessed you are, the more difficult it is to maintain your humility.

That is when true humility will be seen. The difference will be made between a façade of humility and a person humble in the depths of their being: whether or not they lose their stride. The better their results compared to others, the harder it will be for them to believe that, in fact, these results are not due to themselves.

Ultimately, this is our challenge because many of us get stuck or fail on this path of humility and do not manage to travel it to the end. We might start well, but once humility begins to take root, blessings and success will appear in our lives. Many of us forget that this is due to God and the fact that we have done nothing but humble ourselves. This is where many of us falter: success, no matter how small, makes us believe we are important in this world when, in fact, our true value comes from our relationship with God[9].

Therefore, humility is the art mastered by a person who, having conducted a relevant analysis of their life, understands that they are merely dust carried by the wind and that, regardless of their desires, God is the supreme authority, and everything depends on Him.

Why, then, in this present generation, can we no longer be truly humble, or has such a mentality become difficult? The feared enemy of humility is pride, which, by definition, is a dysfunction of the human mind, an ethical and moral dysfunction that individuals cultivate and elevate throughout their lives. Pride is a dysfunction that distorts human optics. It's as if you're wearing glasses that show you the world the way you want it to be and not the way it really is. This dysfunction places a person in an unfortunate situation because they consider themselves self-sufficient and believe their desires are above any moral norms. A proud person is one who cares for no one. They are the person who considers themselves to be above everyone else.

Upon careful analysis, we see that the modern society we live in encourages and educates its individuals to become proud, for the simple reason that proud people will be competitive and willing to compete with each other; therefore, they will be easily manipulated through various mechanisms—be they financial, positional, or status-based. People who are in a lower position can easily be bought if offered a higher management position. This is because people seek recognition, and

[9] Warren, Rick. *The Purpose Driven Life: What on Earth Am I Here For?* Zondervan, 2002.

society educates them to always want more, to take precedence over others, and to maintain a successful image.

Have you ever wondered why, in recent opinion polls, young people often respond that they desire higher positions? You will rarely find someone who says they want to be an average-level person. Don't misunderstand me; it's good to aim high. It's good to want the best for ourselves, but we should become what we have been endowed by the Creator to be on this earth. For example, a person whose body is not anthropometrically configured to be a good swimmer will never be able to compete in Olympic swimming competitions because their body structure will not support them. That's precisely why, in all sporting activities, participants are selected based on their physical abilities.

We must be careful how we educate ourselves and always be ready to conduct a relevant self-analysis, because, unfortunately, today's society has educated us in a direction that favours pride, making it into a tool for mass control and keeping people dependent on the values society promotes.

I pause for a moment to analyse complexes or psychological dysfunctions in our minds that generate and feed pride. Thus, proud people will always have certain complexes: they will either have an inferiority complex—meaning they feel smaller than others but desperately want to be bigger than them—or a superiority complex—they consider themselves to be better than everyone else. Yet neither sees reality clearly anymore and becomes conceited[10].

A proud person will stumble over others,
but a humble person will have no problem
lifting others.

Moreover, a proud person will consider that other people are actually the proud ones. Here lies the greatest distortion of reality that this scourge provides: the lens that hide the way the world truly is will make us see others as proud. In other words, we see in others what we actually are. A proud person will always say about others that they are proud and will refer to themselves as good. In contrast, a humble person will always say about themselves that they have not yet reached a good state and that they need to work more on themselves. A humble person will look at themselves, not at others, whereas a proud person will never look in the mirror to self-analyse but only to judge others, using themselves as a benchmark.

An anomaly I want to clarify (given that it is usually quickly overlooked by researchers) is that as we become more humble, proud people will chastise us for being the proud ones. They do it instinctively because they feel offended. The reality they have built for themselves is challenged by the logic of your humility, and in their desire to defend their image, they will react

---

[10] Burgo, Joseph. *The Narcissist You Know: Defending Yourself Against Extreme Narcissists in an All-About-Me Age.* Touchstone, 2015.

violently. The more you grow in knowledge and rise above others, the more those with an inferiority complex will consider you proud.

There is an expression in the Bible: *"Knowledge puffs up" (1 Corinthians 8:1, NKJV)*. Knowledge puffs up when you don't master it. Too much knowledge puffs up those who do not self-evaluate. In fact, Psalm 1:2 calls those who meditate on the Lord's law, day and night, *happy*. But if you meditate on God's law and fill your mind with knowledge, you will remain with God and you will not feel the need to use knowledge to boast before others. Because God hates pride: *"Whoever secretly slanders his neighbour, Him I will destroy; the one who has a haughty look and a proud heart, him I will not endure" (Psalm 101:5, NKJV)*. *"Everyone proud in heart is an abomination to the Lord; though they join forces, none will go unpunished" (Proverbs 16:5, NKJV)*.

Pride is very dangerous because it brings destruction with it. In Isaiah chapter 14, we are told that even the evil one, whom we call Satan, fell along with a third of God's angels because he was proud. He wanted to surpass the condition for which he was created. Therefore, be careful about what this society prescribes to you; not all of us can become astronauts. Not all of us can become pilots. Not all of us can become doctors. Not all of us can become highly esteemed. Seek to understand what God created you for. Seek to understand your role in this world. Otherwise, you will end up in a place where you will lose your footing.

Before moving forward, I want to analyse some detailed elements that can be misinterpreted upon a cursory glance. There are various ways a person chooses to behave throughout their life, which may or may not rightly be characterised as pride.

There is a difference between the type of pride God hates and the satisfaction or fulfilment (often mistaken for pride) we can feel regarding something well done

---

Let's compare the following verses: *"The fear of the Lord is to hate evil; pride and arrogance and the evil way and the perverse mouth I hate" (Proverbs 8:13, NKJV)* versus *"But let each one examine his own work, and then he will have rejoicing in himself alone, and not in another" (Galatians 6:4, NKJV).*

There is a difference between the two, because one of these is not actually pride, according to the definition in an English dictionary and psychological analysis. Contrary to the opinion of many, who say that Galatians 6 describes a proud man, I believe this is merely the description of a person who is satisfied and simply happy because they achieved what they desired.

For example, when someone is happy because they received the highest grade on an exam, those who received an eight, seven, or six will sit in a corner and look at this person with disdain and judge them as being proud. Perhaps that person is sincerely exuberant and joyful before God, because they achieved a good result, without being proud in the true sense of the word. There is a significant difference between a manifestation that is specific pride—stemming from an inferiority or superiority complex, and from the desire to display oneself—and the pure joy of a person who does not care what others say or do and simply celebrates their success in humility.

Another example is that of parents who are proud of their children and praise them when they have the opportunity to do so. Other people will say they are boastful and proud. It is in our nature to rejoice in the achievements of those dear to us. This is not pride. Pride that makes you show yourself only to humiliate others, pride that makes you try to cover up an inferiority or superiority complex, pride that has distorted your perception of reality is not the same as the happiness that you have accomplished something good. It is not the same as expressing your happiness for loved ones and their achievements. *"Great is my boldness of speech toward you, great is my boasting on your behalf. I am filled with comfort. I am exceedingly joyful in all our tribulation" (2 Corinthians 7:4, NKJV).* The Apostle Paul rejoiced with indescribable joy for others, but he never boasted about himself.

How can we recognise a proud person? What is their profile? What are their characteristics, lest we should follow in their footsteps? Psalm 10:3 (NKJV) provides us with a clear depiction: *"For the wicked boasts of his heart's desire."*

Proud people always highlight their personal achievements, which they attribute exclusively to themselves and which they use to humiliate others. Proud people will always boast, in fact, with their wickedness: *"The wicked [...] mocks and disregards the Lord. [He] says with arrogance: The Lord will not punish! There is no God! [...] He says in his heart: I shall not be moved; I shall never be in adversity. His mouth is full of cursing and deceit and oppression; under his tongue is trouble and iniquity. He sits in the lurking places of the villages; in the secret places, he murders the innocent (Psalm 10:3-4, 6-8, NKJV).*

A proud person sees others as enemies, not as people who need their help and for whom they must sacrifice themselves. A proud person will trample over others, even hurt them, if necessary, to maintain their own ego. Do we have these tendencies? If so, we must immediately assess ourselves carefully.

Do you remember what we learned in the first chapter of our journey? Namely, the first step toward forming a mindset specific to happy people is humility. To recognise our self-failure? Or to be poor in spirit? Pride is the opposite of the spirit of humility that God seeks when He says: *"Blessed are the poor in spirit"* *(Matthew 5:3, NKJV)*. A truly humble person will not think of evil, will not mock, and will not consider themselves omnipotent and self-sufficient, as evidenced in Scripture: *"I shall not be moved; I shall never be in adversity"* *(Psalm 10:4, NKJV)*.

───────● ●───────

The poor in spirit are, first and foremost, sincere because they understand and acknowledge that they need to change themselves, not others.

───────● ●───────

Sometimes we want to change all the people around us, but never ourselves.

Unfortunately, pride will have profound psychological consequences in each of our lives. If they do not act on it in due time, proud people will come to feel insignificant, despite forcing themselves to believe they are important. And they will force themselves to feel important precisely because they feel overlooked, insecure, and unloved. Proud people will feel the need for their life partners to confirm many times a day that they are loved, and this is due to insecurity[11].

These people will find fault in everything and will seek to show that they can do better in every field. A proud person invited to your table will soon show you all the flaws you have in your home, along with all the improvements you need to make.

Proud people are always afraid of being humiliated. They are afraid of appearing vulnerable, they have low self-esteem and impossible standards of perfection. Pride will tell you that you are all-knowing. Do not believe these things. Rather, correct them![12]

Pride has psychological consequences that produce deep wounds and often leave scars, but it also has spiritual consequences. *"Pride will always precede destruction, a fall, a total collapse" (Proverbs 16:18, NKJV).* Be ready to rebuild your life. Be ready to analyse your life and eliminate pride from it because you will end up falling. *"Better to be of a humble spirit*

---

[11] Brown, Brené. *Daring Greatly: How the Courage to Be Vulnerable Transforms the Way We Live, Love, Parent, and Lead.* Avery, 2012.

[12] Brooks, David. *The Road to Character.* Random House, 2015.

with the lowly, than to divide the spoil with the proud" (Proverbs 16:19, NKJV). A humble person will look at themselves and correct certain things, whereas a proud person, as mentioned earlier, will compare themselves to others, always trying to land on their feet.

I now want to direct our attention to an unfortunate manifestation of pride that wreaks havoc in modern society: the tendency of proud people to issue prejudices. Prejudices are those preconceived ideas and opinions that a person forms about other people or a certain thing without actual knowledge of the facts and details concerning them. Prejudices are often imposed through education: we learn them, and we cultivate them, as a result of different influences in our lives[13].

As the etymology suggests, he term *prejudice* is a thought that arises before judging; it derives more from instinct and is then pursued without further analysis[14].

Do you remember Peter, the one who was with the Lord Jesus Christ and was called to be a fisher of men? In the Book of Acts, chapter 10, even though he had a divine mission, Peter initially harboured prejudice against Cornelius and his family, considering them unworthy of receiving divine grace. Similarly, the prophet Jonah initially refused to go to Nineveh, allowing his own prejudice against the city's inhabitants, whom he deemed undeserving of God's mercy, to guide his actions.

---

[13] Banaji, Mahzarin R., and Anthony G. Greenwald. *Blindspot: Hidden Biases of Good People.* Delacorte Press, 2013.

[14] Amodio, D. M., & Cikara, M. (2021). The social neuroscience of prejudice. *Annual Review of Psychology, 72*, pp. 439–469. https://doi.org/10.1146/annurev-psych-010419-050928.

A contemporary example, frequently encountered in our society, is the rejection of someone based on their ethnicity. This kind of behaviour is not just a fleeting act of injustice; it is deeply rooted in the prejudices and stereotypes that have been ingrained in us over time, often unconsciously, by the world around us. These prejudices act as invisible barriers, preventing us from seeing the inherent worth and dignity of each person, who, like us, is created in the image and likeness of God. When we judge others based on their ethnicity, we fail to recognise the rich diversity of God's creation and the unique gifts each person brings to the world. Such attitudes not only harm those we judge but also impoverish our own spiritual lives, limiting our capacity for empathy, understanding, and love.

If not identified, isolated, and eliminated, prejudices will create distance between you and God. They originate in a proud heart that distorts reality through its own filters.

Why should I humble myself in a world where one can only get ahead by pushing others aside or by being as loud as possible? Well, because pride and prejudice are formidable enemies of happiness. Those who fall prey to pride or prejudice will not find happiness, nor will they experience true joy and self-fulfilment. However, humble people, those who have examined themselves and recognised their mistakes, and strive to correct them, will free themselves from the burdens they placed on their own shoulders. They will be ready to step forward into God's plan, thereby rediscovering their happiness.

Chapter 4

❦

Healing Regrets

"Blessed are those who mourn,
for they shall be comforted"
Matthew 5:4 (NKJV).

Having passed through the first antechamber of our journey, where we learned that the authentic path to the mindset of happy people begins with recognising our self-failure, we now reach the **second antechamber**. In this chapter called *Healing Regrets*, we will explore what it means to have genuine regret capable of bringing about a complete correction of life. We will understand what it means to acknowledge our guilt, to repair what we have broken, and why we must strive to change the mindset society has pushed us toward.

When we talk about regret, we refer to a sense of remorse caused by the loss of something or someone or the awareness of having committed a reprehensible act. Regrets begin to appear when we understand and become aware of this loss.[15]

However, are there healing regrets that bring not only pain but also remedy? According to psychological studies, regrets can have beneficial effects, such as learning from mistakes and improving future decisions[16].

To delve deeper into this aspect, we need to focus on the most fundamental aspect of regret, namely, understanding what crying means and its role in our lives. Although it may seem trivial, in the pursuit of happiness, many of us have learned to avoid or accept crying. In many cultures, seeing a man cry is perceived as a sign of weakness, often discouraged by those who wish to be seen as strong. It is essential to analyse these aspects to better understand their impact on us.

Human crying can be analysed from two perspectives:

1. *Natural Crying*: This arises either from physical pain or psychological distress. Since biblical times, the manuscripts that connect us to our cultural roots mention the concept of *"fenteo,"* meaning *"to lament, to cry when you have lost something or someone."* This reaction to pain is present from birth—the first sign of life for a newborn is crying. As we grow, our losses and pains are expressed less through physical crying and

---

[15] Towers, A., Williams, M. N., Hill, S. R., & Philipp, M. C. (2016). What makes for the most intense regrets? Comparing the effects of several theoretical predictors of regret intensity. Frontiers in Psychology, 7, Article 1941. https://doi.org/10.3389/fpsyg.2016.01941.

[16] Roese, N. J. (2005). If Only: How to Turn Regret Into Opportunity. Broadway Books.

more through psychological manifestations, such as anxiety, stress, or inner sadness. We often use expressions like "my heart aches" or "I hurt for you" and cry internally for those around us[17].

2. *Spiritual Crying*: This has both positive and negative valences. In its negative form, it manifests as the cry of iniquity, associated with sinful desires. A relevant biblical example is that of King Ahab, who longed to tears for the vineyards of Naboth, a simple man., Although he had everything he could desire, the king wanted more and the Word of God tells us that *"Ahab went into his house sullen and displeased because of the word which Naboth the Jezreelite had spoken to him; for he had said, 'I will not give you the inheritance of my fathers"* *(1 Kings 21:4, NKJV)*. This episode highlights the negative side of crying, where selfish desires and discontent can lead to suffering and unhappiness.

Do you see the negative spiritual side of crying? It happens when you long for something that does not belong to you and suffer because you cannot have it, when you want more than you are due, when you wish to be something you were not destined to be, and when you want to exceed the condition set for you by your Creator.

---

[17] Landa, A., Fallon, B. A., Wang, Z., Duan, Y., Liu, F., Wager, T. D., Ochsner, K., & Peterson, B. S. (2020). When it hurts even more: The neural dynamics of pain and interpersonal emotions. *Journal of Psychosomatic Research, 128*, 109881. https://doi.org/10.1016/j.jpsychores.2019.109881.

Sin often brings with it false and manipulative crying. Many times, tears may run down our cheeks without us understanding the true motivation behind them. We may come to confuse these tears with a state of genuine repentance or humility, even though they are caused by selfish desires or sins. This mentality was also described in the Eastern culture to which we have access by reading the Bible: *"the sorrow of the world produces death,"* but *"godly sorrow produces repentance" (2 Corinthians 7:10, NKJV)*. In other words, when regret is genuine and generated by the awareness of our mistakes, it leads to correcting errors and healing the soul. Conversely, regret born out of envy for others' possessions is a sin that will erode the soul and amplify suffering.

———————•—•———————

Spiritual crying, in its positive valence, can be motivated by genuine regret that arises when we become aware of our mistakes and their consequences. It urges us to do everything possible to correct the errors[18].

———————•—•———————

To understand the difference between positive and negative regrets, we can compare two situations: a thief may cry out of frustration at being caught, but the same thief, understanding

---

[18] Matarazzo, O., Abbamonte, L., Greco, C., Pizzini, B., & Nigro, G. (2021). Regret and other emotions related to decision-making: Antecedents, appraisals, and phenomenological aspects. *Frontiers in Psychology, 12*, Article 783248.

the gravity of his actions, may come to cry not because he was caught but because he sincerely regrets his actions.

There is a fundamental difference between positive spiritual crying – which connects us to reality and inspires us to change – and negative crying, which pushes us to act only to calm our conscience without truly correcting errors. Understanding these nuances can help us better navigate the complexity of our emotions and cultivate regrets that lead to healing and personal growth.

Reflecting on the idea of regret, let us return to the divine wisdom taught by the Saviour Jesus Christ, who offers us a clear perspective on how we should approach life and acknowledge the mistakes of our modern mentality: *"Blessed are those who mourn, for they shall be comforted" (Matthew 5:4, NKJV)*. This logically follows the previous verse: *"Blessed are the poor in spirit... (those who have understood their state)" (Matthew 5:3, NKJV)*. We notice here the emphasis on sincere regret, experienced by those who recognise their mistakes and genuinely wish to correct things.

Authentic regret is not just a form of self-condemnation, but rather a recognition of the negative impact of our actions on others and on our relationship with God. This type of regret prompts us to seek reconciliation and take active steps to eliminate errors and repair damaged relationships. True regret comes from a deep understanding of the consequences of our actions and a sincere desire to correct the errors, not from an attitude of false repentance, expressed only because tradition dictates it or in order to obtain easy forgiveness.

It is important to clarify the difference between genuine and superficial regret. Genuine regret is fuelled by the awareness of the mistake and the desire to make real changes in our lives. In contrast, superficial regret can be a mechanical reaction, a kind of ritual emptied of meaning, which does not bring about inner change. People who feel genuine regret are those who acknowledge that they have hurt their fellow beings and have damaged their relationship with God. They do not manifest their repentance through mere outward gestures, but through a real change of heart and mind[19].

To illustrate this aspect, let us consider the concept of repentance, a term frequently used in Christian culture but often misapplied. Repentance, in its traditional sense, derives from the Slavic word "pocaianie," which literally means to regret and turn away from wrongdoing. However, this definition leaves room for imitative or mechanical behaviours that do not reflect the real and profound change of heart that true repentance demands. Many may repent before others without an inner change, and this repentance is often just a façade with hidden motives.

In the biblical context, the term used is "metanoia," which translates to "the renewal of the mind". Metanoia involves a profound process of inner change, where we confront our

---

[19] Roese, N. J. (2005). *If Only: How to Turn Regret Into Opportunity*. Broadway Books.

mistakes, realise how we have aggrieved God, and then sincerely repent for what we have done.

Unfortunately, in our culture, repentance is often preached as a set of external actions, considering that visible manifestations, such as crying or other gestures of contrition, are sufficient to obtain forgiveness. This approach can suggest that there is no need to deeply understand your mistakes; instead, it is enough to express your emotions. However, true repentance requires an inner transformation, which involves understanding and confronting the truth about your situation.

This transformation is not a simple act of remorse but a commitment to live a better life in accordance with God's will[20].

The process of authentic repentance requires more than simple outward gestures. It begins with acknowledging our mistakes and continues with sincere efforts to change our behaviour. It means committing to a journey of self-awareness and transformation, which helps us improve our relationship with God and our fellow human beings. It means seeking to understand why we have erred and making the necessary changes to prevent repeating the same errors.

---

[20] Strong, J. (1890). *Strong's Exhaustive Concordance of the Bible*. Public Domain. Provides definitions and uses of biblical terms, including metanoia.

Authentic repentance cannot be rushed in our spiritual journey on this earth. It happens at the right time, after we have gone through the important stages of introspection and understanding. To truly change our mind and behaviour, we must be confronted with the truth, to understand what we have done wrong, to realise who we are, and to learn what we must do to correct the errors. This involves a process of self-analysis and self-education, which helps us understand the truth or reality about ourselves and act in accordance with the divine will.

But why is it so important to understand the truth? The answer comes from our cultural and spiritual heritage, from the Judeo-Christian belief that emphasises the importance of truth in the process of reconciliation with God and calibrating the mind to regain happiness. The Apostle Paul tells us: *"Therefore, having been justified by faith, we have peace with God through our Lord Jesus Christ" (Romans 5:1, NKJV)*. Being justified by faith means being right before God based on real and not invented data and facts about our lives. When a person changes after being confronted with the truth, they enter a state of harmony and reconciliation with God and their fellow beings.

Interestingly, in Hebrew, the meaning of *shalom*, usually translated as *peace* or *truce*, is rather closer to *being whole, being complete*. This peace goes beyond the mere absence of conflict; it involves restoring relationships and personal wholeness. The ancient Hebrews used the term shalom not only to describe the absence of war but also to describe a state of integrity and completeness, both personally and communally. This peace involved reconciliation with God and the restoration of broken relationships[21].

However, in our daily life, we often approach faith with a selfish mentality: "Lord, if You do this for me, I will give You this." This approach reduces faith to a commercial exchange, where we try to negotiate divine favours in exchange for our promises.

———————•—•————————

But true faith cannot be conditioned or negotiated. It involves an unconditional commitment to God and an authentic relationship with Him[22].

———————•—•————————

How did we get to this conditional mentality? We have reduced faith to a series of rituals or traditions inherited from our ancestors, without it being accompanied by a profound understanding or personal commitment. Many practice faith as a mere tradition without exploring or delving into its true meaning. This perspective limits our potential, causing us to be content with less than our original purpose. Moreover, not understanding the meaning of repentance (as a renewal of the mind) and faith has led to the trivialisation of contemporary Christianity. Being "repentant" or "faithful" is often perceived as archaic or outdated. It is an injustice, because repentance

---

[21] Woodley, Randy. *Shalom and the Community of Creation: An Indigenous Vision*. Eerdmans, 2012.

[22] Lewis, C.S. *Mere Christianity*. HarperOne, 2001.

comes from the word *metanoia*, which signifies an enlightened mind capable of transformation and reflection on God. But because we have failed to represent this divine light in the world, society has marginalised us, viewing us as outsiders.

Another key aspect that needs mentioning is that we have transformed faith into a set of personal beliefs, without realising that this is, in fact, the definition of a personal and profound relationship with God. We have come to represent it only as knowledge about God, not personal knowledge of Him. It is like knowing facts about historical figures, such as Albert Einstein, without having a personal relationship with them. Similarly, many Christians believe they know God because they know things about Him, but do not have a personal and transformative relationship with Him.

Real faith involves a psychological and spiritual contract with the divine, where understanding and respecting His laws demonstrate our commitment to Him. As it is written in James 2:17-18 (NKJV) *"Thus also faith by itself, if it does not have works, is dead". But someone will say, 'You have faith, and I have works.' Show me your faith without your works, and I will show you my faith by my works"*. Faith must manifest through concrete actions, not just declarations. Philanthropists can do good deeds without religious motives, but authentic faith inspires genuine actions that reflect God's will.

In his epistle, the apostle James emphasises: *"You believe that there is one God. You do well. Even the demons believe— and tremble! But do you want to know, O foolish man, that faith without works is dead?" (James 2:19-20, NKJV)*. Here, the difference between mere belief and real faith is clear. The demons acknowledge the existence of God but do not have a relationship with Him. They tremble because they know the day of judgment awaits them but have no commitment to Him. So it is with faith that has been replaced by personal and customised opinions, to the detriment of an authentic relationship with God.

Instead of mechanical imitation, authentic repentance is based on sincere faith and the commitment to live in accordance with the divine will. It is not just a confession of sin but a commitment to truly change life and reflect God's image in our world.

Authentic repentance is not a mere act of sterile acknowledgment of sin to escape punishment. It involves a deep understanding of the impact of our actions and a sincere desire to repair the relationship with God.

Why have we reached such a superficial mentality in a world so advanced intellectually and technologically? We are part of a society that dictates how we should think, behave, and desire. We live in a world that values noise more than music, darkness more than light, and has sacrificed ethics and morality on the altar of social conformity. We have become prisoners of a society that has legalised nonsense and pushed us to conform to pre-established models, emptied of truth and meaning.

It is crucial to return to the true essence of faith and repentance, to seek to understand God's will and live in accordance with it. Only through an authentic relationship with the divine can we find true peace, which brings integrity and restoration into our lives. This search for truth and reconciliation with God is what can free us from the chains of society and lead us to a life full of meaning and spiritual fulfilment.

In conclusion, authentic regret, repentance, and faith are fundamental elements of the spiritual life that help us correct our errors and live in harmony with the divine will. Through a deep understanding of these concepts, we can overcome the superficiality and trivialisation of modern society and live a life that reflects the true values and ideals of Christianity.

Before bringing this chapter to an end, let us consolidate what we have learned so far and reflect on the example of two well-known historical figures. One is David, the great king of Israel, who recognised his failure and transformed after committing a sin that marked his life. The other is Saul, an opportunistic man who only wanted to impress others without truly changing the essence of his being. After committing adultery and murder, David was confronted with his sin by the prophet Nathan. Instead of defending himself or minimising his actions, David acknowledged his guilt and sincerely sought repentance. Psalm 51 is a testament to his genuine regret and desire to change: *"Create in me a clean heart, O God, and renew a steadfast spirit within me" (Psalm 51:10, NKJV).*

Saul, on the other hand, demonstrated false repentance. When confronted with his disobedience to divine commands, he tried to justify his actions and maintain his image before the people. Unlike David, Saul did not manifest a sincere desire for change, and his lack of authentic regret ultimately led to his downfall.

These examples show us the importance of genuine repentance and real regret in our lives.

In 1 Samuel, chapter 15, we see King Saul before Judge Samuel, who asks him directly why he erred, taking on the role of priest. Saul expresses regret, but only as a facade: *"I have sinned, for I have transgressed the commandment of the Lord and your words, because I feared the people and obeyed their voice. Now therefore, please pardon my sin, and return with me, that I may worship the Lord"* (1 Samuel 15:24-25, NKJV). Saul said again: *"I have sinned; yet honour me now, please, before the elders of my people and before Israel, and return with me, that I may worship the Lord your God"* (1 Samuel 15:30, NKJV).

What do we notice here? A type of regret that resembles the one many of us have: *"Lord, I have sinned because I have also transgressed Your command."* We seek excuses. Saul feared the people. *"Lord, I did it because the serpent deceived me,"* said Eve (Genesis 3:13, NKJV). *"Lord, I did it because the woman You created gave me to eat,"* said Adam (Genesis 3:12, NKJV). "Lord, I did it because the temptation was too great for me," you might say, even though it is written that *no temptation is greater than your power (1 Corinthians 10:13,*

NKJV). Thus, we forget that those who excuse themselves accuse themselves.

We are often like Saul, always seeking ways to enjoy life and God at the same time, dependent on social formulas and prescriptions, telling ourselves that "it works this way too" because God loves us anyway. Saul repented only as a façade, seeking to impress. In your case, have you passed through the first antechamber, or have you sought tricks and shortcuts to gain direct access to the second?

A person of Saul's calibre will always want to be perceived by others as honest, not because they appreciate honesty, but because they want attention, due to not having killed their ego. A person who sincerely regrets what they have done no longer looks at themselves, but at the one they have hurt and seeks to make amends. Why did Saul want to reconcile in the eyes of the world and then worship with Samuel? Because when you are overwhelmed by sin and do not want to rid yourself of it, you want to be carried by someone else, to be carried on their shoulders and pushed from behind. However, there is a much clearer profile of authentic believers, those who are not only convinced that God exists but actually believe in Him.

They are the ones who regret not because they were caught with sin but because they have aggrieved their Creator.

Returning to King David; yet another king, but this time declared to be *"a man after God's own heart"* (1 Samuel 13:14; Acts 13:22, NKJV), a man who sinned much more severely than Saul. The Scriptures show us that David was a special man who understood at one point that sin separated him from God: *"For I acknowledge my transgressions, and my sin is always before me. Against You, You only, have I sinned, and done this evil in Your sight—that You may be found just when You speak, and blameless when You judge"* (Psalm 51:3-4, NKJV). In other words: "Lord, if You erase me from the face of the earth, I do not blame You. I understand what I have done. I am entirely responsible for what I have done. Lord, I have sinned!" David continues in this psalm: *"Behold, I was brought forth in iniquity, and in sin, my mother conceived me. Behold, You desire truth in the inward parts, and in the hidden part, You will make me to know wisdom"* (Psalm 51:5-6, NKJV).

Do you notice the difference between the two approaches? Saul asked Samuel to accompany him as a forerunner before the Lord, hoping that if the Lord saw Samuel, He would look favourably upon Saul. In contrast, David laments his sin and does so personally. He no longer looks left or right and asks God to open his mind. He does not need support but wants to go to the source because he understands he needs transformation: *"Purge me with hyssop, and I shall be clean; wash me, and I shall be whiter than snow. Make me hear joy and gladness, that the bones You have broken may rejoice"* (Psalm 51:7-8, NKJV).

Looking at these two examples, we understand that an authentic believer, once stripped of self, realises that their state is caused solely by their own mistakes and takes responsibility for their wrong decisions and actions, without blaming God's lack of indulgence.

How many of us argue with God, reproaching Him, like the disciples of old: *"Teacher, do You not care that we are perishing?" (Mark 4:38, NKJV)*, after we have previously declared that God incarnated in the person of the Lord Jesus? We reproach the Creator for the very key element for which He came to earth: precisely because He cares, precisely because He is compassionate; in other words, He is empathetic with us. Letting ourselves be carried away by temptation, we say things that hurt Him even more.

I conclude this chapter with the thoughts of the great King David: *"Create in me a clean heart, O God, and renew a steadfast spirit within me" (Psalm 51:10, NKJV).*

***

*** **This is where repentance comes in: you cannot place a new and steadfast spirit in a person until you have stripped them of their sinful spirit.** ***

***

God will never place His diamonds in a handful of stones gathered from the dark marshes of this world and the desolate places of sin. If you want to hold God's diamonds in your hand, then cast away all the worthless stones you have now. Allow yourself to be stripped of yourself, and God will fill you with His Spirit.

Chapter 5

Sine Cera

"Let not mercy and truth forsake you; bind them around your neck, write them on the tablet of your heart" (Proverbs 3:3, NKJV).

The concept of faithfulness originates from the Hebrew word *emet*, which means, simply put, "truth." In this context, the motto "Let not mercy and truth forsake us" suggests that we must keep kindness and truth close to our hearts and minds. These should become the essence of each of our lives. If we demonstrate a divine character toward others, we must be honest with ourselves.

The title of this chapter has its origin in Roman culture, which we have adopted in the history of our people. Sine Cera, in Latin, means "without wax" and is the etymological basis of the word "sincerity."

In the past, Sine Cera was a term used to describe people who were not duplicitous, who did not seek unmerited benefits, and who were genuine and honest[23].

From an etymological perspective, Sine Cera comes from a historical period when the pottery industry was highly valued. The potter worked the clay, shaped it beautifully, and then placed it in a hot oven to harden the vessel, giving it the shine and durability needed to be used in the household or in the fashion and beauty industry of the time. Then, as now, industry workers used little tricks. Sometimes, the vessels had defects, showing cracks caused by the oven's temperature being too high or too low. Perhaps the clay was not well-prepared, or the vessel was not positioned correctly in the oven. In any case, unsightly cracks appeared, making the vessel inadequate. A trick used by potters was to hide the cracks by sealing them with wax, which they masked with a thin layer of glue mixed with paint, thus creating a temporary fix for the cracks. Unfortunately, this method was only effective until the housewife placed the vessel in the oven, waiting to taste the much-desired dish. The wax could not withstand high temperatures, and the valuable contents seeped through the cracks in the hot oven, being quickly consumed.

---

[23] Magill, R. Jay Jr. *Sincerity: How a Moral Ideal Born Five Hundred Years Ago Inspired Religious Wars, Modern Art, Hipster Chic, and the Curious Notion that We All Have Something to Say (No Matter How Dull)*. W. W. Norton & Company, 2012.

Starting from this analogy, the Word of God urges us to be people without wax. Just as someone desires a wax-free vessel, so God desires that we all be sincere.

We have learned in the early chapters that happy people are those who have understood, above all, the importance of recognising their own failures. They have already passed the first antechamber of our journey, where they examined their humility, assessed their pride and prejudices, and did their best so that when they move on to the second antechamber – that of healing regrets – they come prepared and ready to be transformed.

We will not be able to move on to the third antechamber – which we will discuss in detail in the next chapter – until we sincerely regret the mistakes we made, without hiding anything and without trying to fill the unsightly cracks we have with the wax of untruth.

Sincerity is a fundamental human trait characterised by the absence of pretence or deceit, marked by loyalty and candour. It is primarily a quality directed inwardly, focusing on our own self-assessment rather than on interactions with others. In essence, sincerity involves a genuine self-reflection and evaluation of our own thoughts, feelings, and actions.

Often, a person cannot find happiness precisely because their transformation is neither complete nor sincere.

Throughout our life, we have all sought to intervene in this process of transformation and adjust it according to our own whims.

The question you might ask now is, "How can I too, benefit from a true transformation?" The answer is clear and concise: true and total transformation comes through understanding and accepting the truth.

But what is truth? Understanding this question is essential for calibrating our sincerity. Truth is a concordance between our knowledge and objective reality. It is the faithful reflection of the reality that surrounds us. To acquire this character trait called sincerity, meaning to be "without wax," we must understand what truth is. Then, we will discover together how we can incorporate this truth into our own character and how we can calibrate our sincerity in truth.

The diametric opposite of truth is untruth, not lies. Lies are the mechanism by which truth is transformed into untruth; it is the path or intrigue through which truth is systematically deconstructed and then recreated[24].

What value does truth hold in a world where we are told that everything is relative and that our knowledge is only partial?

Let's look at the following illustration that shows how easily untruth can be transformed, manipulated, and presented with emotional embellishments, so as to look like pure truth.

---

[24] Ariely, Dan. *The Honest Truth About Dishonesty: How We Lie to Everyone–Especially Ourselves.* HarperCollins, 2012.

Have you heard of outlawry? Traditionally speaking, the outlawry of yore is presented today as a good thing because when they stole from the rich and gave to the poor, they did something good, bringing justice to all. However, if we take another look at the word in any explanatory dictionary, we notice that outlaws had no positive, ethical, or moral value and could not be associated with truth because outlaws were those who opposed social order and laws. They lived alone or in bands in the forests and engaged in robbing those they considered wealthy. In an attempt to absolve themselves, they later helped the poor — a way to heal a sin by committing another, a way to correct a mistake by making two more. This type of Christian outlawry, this modern outlawry, can be found and circulates freely through many of the apparently ethical and moral Christian philosophies of our times.

In contrast, the Bible draws our attention to the fact that although we were once darkness—not just in darkness (meaning we generated the darkness)—now we are light in the Lord *(Ephesians 5:8, NKJV).*

We must walk and manifest in this world as if we are light. For the fruit of divine light in our world is goodness, righteousness, and truth.

Goodness is always expressed toward others. Righteousness is expressed in both directions: both toward yourself and toward others, and truth becomes, practically, the corollary, that beautiful aura that encompasses both goodness and righteousness.

Although attractive, feigned sincerity, this chameleonic tendency by which we deceive others by displaying an apparently good image, is actually a trap of death. An example I offer is the phenomenon of bioluminescence found in the marine environment. Marine creatures often use bioluminescence to attract prey, which they then crush and cut to pieces.

To understand why sincerity must be authentic and based on truth, and not on the mechanisms of modern relativism – where truth is considered just a personal opinion – we must analyse how many of us transform truth into lies to make our lives more comfortable.

Lying is so present in our lives that we often do not even notice it. Studies by developmental psychologists show that lying appears in children's lives starting at the age of two. This ability is seen as a sign of cognitive sophistication because it requires an understanding of the beliefs and intentions of others[25]. Children often use crying and their delicate appearance (which they know how to exploit to the fullest) to deceive us.

Lying has become a common aspect of human behaviour. Research indicates that most people lie at least once a day,

---

[25] Lee, Kang. "Little Liars: Development of Verbal Deception in Children." *Child Development Perspectives*, vol. 7, no. 2, 2013, pp. 91–96. https://doi.org/10.1111/cdep.12023.

often in minor or socially acceptable ways. Lies range from small, courteous ones to more significant deceptions and are integrated into daily interactions, where false statements deliberately distort the truth, transforming reality into untruth[26].

A particular form of untruth is religious lying. This is a complex form of self-manipulation by which a person chooses to comfort themselves, telling themselves that they are in accordance with God's will, even when there is a significant discrepancy between what they say and what they do.

What we think is not the same as what we declare, believe, or do. At one point, the Saviour addressed the scribes and Pharisees of the time, telling them that their way of life did not indicate that they had God as their Father but rather the devil (John 8:44) because the devil is the father of lies, and they had often been found to be liars[27].

I want to bring up a term that highlights the fact that religious lying can be a barrier on the path to self-discovery: opportunism. People often become opportunists, manifesting a lack of principles to satisfy their personal interests. According

[26] Feldman, Robert S. "Liar, Liar: Deception in Everyday Life." *American Scientist*, vol. 94, no. 6, 2006, pp. 515-517. https://www.jstor.org/stable/27858701.

[27] Tavris, Carol, and Elliot Aronson. *Mistakes Were Made (But Not by Me): Why We Justify Foolish Beliefs, Bad Decisions, and Hurtful Acts.* Mariner Books, 2015.

to the definition of the term, opportunists choose to adopt and apply principles and opinions suitable to the moment, depending on circumstances. In a chameleonic style, either one way or another, opportunists are ready to change their beliefs according to the preferences of their audience or those they interact with. With such reactions, faith will no longer be anchored in truth, and this will prevent us from finding happiness.

If we take a look at our lives, we may notice that our sincerity is no longer authentic because truth, which should be at the foundation of our life, has been restructured and transformed through lies into untruth.

Here are seven types of lies you might find in your life. If not identified, analysed, and stopped, these lies can obstruct and damage your ability to be a sincere person; they will cloud your mind and give you a duplicitous mentality. In the end, you will end up being insincere with yourself.

1. **Error** is a lie that occurs by mistake, and the one who lied believes with every bone in their body that they have spoken the truth. Later, reality will prove the opposite: that which was said is not true. Therefore, we must be very careful in how we express ourselves and, before making a statement, we need to make sure we rely on the truth.

2. **Lying by omission** involves intentionally avoiding relevant information, preferring those more digestible to the interlocutors and less risky for oneself. Lying by omission does not involve inventing stories but simply omitting certain details from a reality or event that has

already happened. It is, by definition, a passive deception that generates less guilt in the mind of the person using it, compared to a blatant and exaggerated lie[28]. Many of us resort to omission, believing it to be acceptable and thinking we have not lied. We use omission because we feel less guilty than if we were to lie outright.

3. **Lying by restructuring or distorting the context.** We often encounter people who want to convey their message but do so sarcastically. They intentionally change the identity of the characters or convey a message in a humorous style. This is a lie because the interlocutor is misled, and the message is transmitted as a joke[29]. The truth must be told with elegance and tact, not through sarcasm or restructuring reality.

4. **Denial** is one of the most dangerous forms of lying because it involves refusing to acknowledge the truth. Denial can be intrapersonal and represents an especially dangerous state of lying because the individual refuses to accept reality. This form of lying frequently occurs in people who have experienced trauma and refuse to accept that their problem truly exists. For these people, healing will be difficult, and hope will seem distant because, as long as they do not acknowledge reality as it is and do not accept the existence of the problem, they will not have the capacity to move forward. In our case,

---

[28] Bok, Sissela. *Lying: Moral Choice in Public and Private Life.* Vintage Books, 1999
[29] Gibbs, Raymond W. *The Poetics of Mind: Figurative Thought, Language, and Understanding.* Cambridge University Press, 1994

we will remain stuck in the second antechamber, where the tears of regret will no longer bring healing but will lead to finding extenuating circumstances and unjustified excuses, constantly asking for mercy[30].

Denial can be both interpersonal and intrapersonal. This form of denial is also delicate because we deny the truth communicated by others. We find ways to deny what others say, transforming truth into falsehood.

5. **Minimising the experiences of others, their psychological state, or a factual situation**, is a form of lying that involves presenting the consequences of a mistake in a distorted manner and is always accompanied by a fundamental attribution error. Minimisation involves intentionally downplaying the effects or scope of your mistake on others to save your image. It is the belief that what you did is small and insignificant compared to the actual effects. However, if the same situation were to happen to you, you would consider it a cataclysm. Minimisation involves using distorted judgment to escape blame.

6. **Exaggeration of information** is a form of deception in which a person presents a situation or problem as much more serious or significant than it actually is. This lie often involves inflating facts or overestimating details to create a distorted version of reality. By exaggerating, the person tries to manipulate others'

---

[30] Tavris, Carol, and Elliot Aronson. *Mistakes Were Made (But Not by Me): Why We Justify Foolish Beliefs, Bad Decisions, and Hurtful Acts*. Mariner Books, 2015.

perceptions and emotions, provoking unjustified stress, fear, or anger. Exaggeration can be used deliberately to mislead or harm others, making them believe that circumstances are much more severe than they are, leading to exaggerated emotional reactions and conflicts. This tactic can be used to gain sympathy, avoid responsibility, or gain advantage in social or professional situations. Over time, such exaggerations can erode trust and credibility, as others may eventually recognise the pattern of distortion and become sceptical of the person's claims[31].

7. **Fabrication of information** is a complex type of lie in which a person deliberately invents a false story to gain a personal advantage. This type of deception requires the ability to construct a credible narrative by mixing fictitious details with real elements. Fabrication occurs in various contexts, from interpersonal relationships to the professional environment and public communication, being used to manipulate others' perceptions and emotions.

The consequences of fabricating information can be severe because once the truth is discovered, credibility and trust are often compromised. Those who fabricate lies risk losing their reputation and personal or professional relationships and may face legal or ethical implications. This phenomenon underscores the importance of integrity and truth in communication,

---

[31] DePaulo, Bella M. "The Many Faces of Lies." *The Social Psychology of Good and Evil*, edited by Arthur G. Miller, 2nd ed., The Guilford Press, 2016, pp. 227–248.

highlighting the risks associated with deliberate lies in a society where information is easily accessible and verifiable[32].

If we choose to examine ourselves carefully, we will likely discover the presence of one or more forms of lying in our lives. When they exist, our sincerity as a character trait suffers. Our life becomes a vessel whose cracks are not repaired with clay but with wax – a cheaper and more convenient solution.

Unfortunately, the wax of untruth melts easily in the fire of trials.

This is the major challenge for those seeking happiness: as long as our sincerity is not based on truth, we will remain stuck in the antechamber of regrets. If our sincerity is just a wax mask for the cracks in our vessel, we will end up deceiving ourselves.

The Bible urges us to be people who believe without doubt, *"to be renewed in the spirit of your mind and put on the new man ... of a righteousness and holiness that only truth can give" (Ephesians 4:23-24, NKJV).* The Apostle Paul continues, saying, *"Let each one of you speak truth with his neighbour" (Ephesians 4:25, NKJV).*

---

[32] Vrij, Aldert. *Detecting Lies and Deceit: Pitfalls and Opportunities.* Wiley, 2008.

When we become accustomed to lying to each other, we quickly become people who lie to themselves. A relevant aspect is the lie caused by cognitive dissonance. When a problem arises in our minds, we quickly seek mitigating circumstances to resolve it. Imagine, for instance, that you went to a shop to buy a product; it looks extraordinary in the store, where the seller knows how to capture your interest, but when you get home, you are disappointed. The product's shine is no longer the same, and your enthusiasm has faded. At that moment, cognitive dissonance intervenes, and your mind will generate various justifications, such as that you must have purchased it at a better price or that it will be useful in the future. Thus, your mind tries to reduce the tension and align your perceptions.

The Bible advises us to be careful, to walk as wise people, and to avoid being *"drunk with wine"* (Ephesians 5:15, 18, NKJV). Originating from ancient Jewish and Greek culture, this expression signifies avoiding deceptive philosophies that can lead us astray.

Understanding that lies are a mechanism that transforms truth into untruth, and knowing that truth is the foundation of sincerity, we ask ourselves: how can we perceive pure truth, both regarding ourselves and others? A suggestive proverb says, "If the eye does not see, neither does the heart grieve." For example, a child visiting grandparents knocks over a vase that chips and breaks. To solve the problem, the child turns the vase so that the crack is oriented toward the wall, making it invisible. As long as the defect is not observed, other people are none the wiser. However, the error or the damage persists, which also lingers in the mind of the child who committed the mistake.

Why do we tend to make such adjustments to reality to hide our behaviour? Why are we tempted to mask even our regrets with a lie? This happens because the mind controls us, and the psychological factors that dominate our thinking urge us to contort the truth. We often have the desire to justify everything we do[33]. We use prejudices and consider ourselves more virtuous than those around us. Additionally, we often commit the fundamental attribution error: when things go well, we take all the credit, but when they don't, we blame others. We also display confirmation bias: we stubbornly search for arguments and reasons to support our point of view, refusing to correct our mistakes[34].

To understand the pure truth about ourselves and avoid cognitive errors such as confirmation bias or fundamental attribution error, we must eliminate personal justifications. This can be achieved through several mechanisms:

1. The true mirror is external, not internal feedback.

It is essential to pay attention to our surrounding reality and to how we perceive ourselves. This reflection should be guided by the Word of God, and the opinions of those who anchor their lives in God should have value. Only through God's

---

[33] Von Hippel, William, and Robert Trivers. "The Evolution and Psychology of Self-Deception." *Behavioral and Brain Sciences*, vol. 34, no. 1, 2011, pp. 1-56.

[34] Tversky, A., & Kahneman, D. (1981). The framing of decisions and the psychology of choice. Science, 211(4481), pp. 453-458. https://doi.org/10.1126/science.7455683).

lens can we understand the truth: *"The statutes of the Lord are right, rejoicing the heart; the commandment of the Lord is pure, enlightening the eyes" (Psalm 19:8, NKJV)*. Additionally, Psalm 119:5 (NKJV) tells us that Scripture is the light that guides our steps.

———•———

The Bible acts as a mirror that reveals the sins in our lives, and to discover the truth, we only need to look into it. It represents humanity's moral and ethical code, guiding us toward what God's Word says.

———•———

2. Truth is gradually revealed through divine wisdom.

Imagine a dark cave full of treasures but also snakes, rats, bats, and other frightening creatures. If you explore this cave with a flashlight, looking for treasures, you will feel much more comfortable than if someone were to suddenly turn on a strong light, revealing all those creatures. This sudden light might make you uncomfortable, as it would clearly show you everything happening around you. That's how the Word of God works. Through the Holy Spirit, He diligently comes and gradually illuminates those places in our lives where we have made mistakes, so we can correct them gradually, ensuring permanent correction. If we were suddenly and brutally exposed to our true image, we might never want to listen again.

3. Truth is always revealed through God's people.

There is a proverb that says: "Tell me who you associate with, and I'll tell you who you are." If you want to find out the truth about yourself so you know exactly what kind of person you are, remember: seek to look in the mirror of God's Word, understand that truth is revealed through Him, and get closer to God's people. *"Confess your sins to one another and pray for one another so that you may be healed" (James 5:16, NKJV).* Help each other: this is a fundamental principle. When you have a trusted person to discuss things with, a personal coach, or a mentor, things will go much better. However, to achieve this, we must first solve the issue of pride and prejudices, which we discussed in previous chapters.

Truth can be painful, isn't it? You might wonder how to cultivate the sincere regret that brings about healing but does not seek the attention of others. This is the strategy each of us must adopt. As the light reveals unpleasant truths in our minds, we may tend to victimise ourselves because the truth hurts. To avoid this and use the truth for real transformation and healing, we must first acknowledge our condition without making excuses.

———————• •———————

Train your mind not to find justifications!
Like David, tell God and yourself: "For I
know my transgressions, and my sin is
always before me" (Psalm 51:3, NKJV).

———————• •———————

Secondly, carefully weigh the effects and consequences of lying on your own life. We often use lies to turn truth into untruth because we no longer recognise their effects on our lives. Our sincerity turns into a kind of religious chameleon because we no longer understand whom we are harming; thus, we cancel our hope and chance to live. *"Against You, You only, have I sinned and done what is evil in Your sight, so that You are justified when You speak and blameless when You judge"* (Psalm 51:4, NKJV).

The third step is to carefully weigh the effects and consequences of lying, not just on your life but also on the lives of others. An insincere person who uses lies not only harms themselves but also others, who will suffer. They will suffer because of the untruth you told. If you examine yourself closely and find lies in your behaviour, if you realise that you are not an honest person but rather insincere and duplicitous, with a chameleon-like nature, you should know that, at some point, just as Abel's blood cried out from the ground to God, the people you deceived in the past, the people you deceive now, the people whose expectations you betray will ask their Creator why you did this. He will reveal your deeds to them. You will then feel ashamed. Avoid such a state and enjoy an honest attitude.

Fourth, we can cultivate sincere regret by analysing how our sins affect our Lord Jesus Christ, especially after He sacrificed Himself for us. It is written: *"And if someone asks Him, 'What are these wounds on Your hands?' He will answer, 'I received them in the house of those who loved Me'" (Zechariah 13:6, NKJV).*

The general idea is that Lord Jesus died for our sins. He was not crucified for sins in general or for the idea of sin, but for our individual mistakes and sins. Otherwise, there would be no justice in God. Therefore, every sin and mistake you make creates a scar in His soul. What hurt our Creator the most, when He was with His disciples on the stormy sea, was the expression thrown out hastily and thoughtlessly: *"Lord, don't You care that we are perishing?" (Mark 4:38).* The most likely answer on that difficult night was: **"I came precisely for this reason, precisely because I care!"**

Because the truth hurts, seek to cultivate in yourself sincere regret, a source of healing. Do not seek excuses and evasive reasons. The truth will set you free! The truth will bring you what lies never will: you will find solace! Only when we regret our mistakes and sins will we receive healing.

It is written: *"Come to Me, all you who are weary and burdened, and I will give you rest. Take My yoke upon you and learn from Me, for I am gentle and humble in heart; and you will find rest for your souls. For My yoke is easy and My burden is light" (Matthew 11:28-30, NKJV).*

How, then, can you find solace through sincerity? Ask God for forgiveness, complete forgiveness, as David, the psalmist, once asked: *"Have mercy on me, O God, according to Your lovingkindness; according to the greatness of Your compassion, blot out my transgressions" (Psalm 51:1, NKJV).* In the same Psalm 51 (NKJV), David said: *"Wash me thoroughly from my iniquity and cleanse me from my sin"* and *"Create in me a clean heart, O God, and renew a steadfast spirit within me"* (verses 2, 10).

Ask God for a new and clean mind, one where lies no longer have a place, a mind that is sincere, "without wax."

Therefore, ask God to transform you into a new person. After that, all other things will fall into place.

We all are and will be tested, and we all will be examined. Therefore, I advise you to develop a sincere mindset, to understand how to practise the truth. This mindset should be inspired by the wisdom left to us by Solomon: *"Remove the dross from the silver, and a vessel will come forth for the silversmith" (Proverbs 25:4, NKJV).* Once the metals have been melted under the inferno of temperature, their density will bring out the dross, dirt, and impurities. These will be easily collected by the expert, set aside, and the precious metal will be truly valued.

Chapter 6

The Art of Gentleness in a Selfish World

"Blessed are the meek, for they shall inherit the earth" (Matthew 5:5, NKJV).

We take another step on our spiritual journey, entering the **third chamber**, where we will learn that God desires us to master the art of gentleness in an often-selfish world. Living morally in today's world may seem like a myth that is difficult to comprehend, particularly for this contemporary generation, that is accustomed to an often-distorted thinking that we feel deeply within our souls.

We live in a turbulent world, under the threat of war, of nuclear, economic, and social crises. It is a world in which we segregate rather than unite. Although theoretically we claim to be one body, we shy away from each other; we seek to elevate only ourselves, as we are driven by the desire to rise higher.

Sometimes, we use any means to get what we want, without caring about others.

Let us now consider the following questions: What did the Creator ask of us from the very beginning, when He placed us in this world? What does He ask us to demonstrate to the world? And how can we achieve this?

From the outset of answering these questions, we observe that we, as humans, have begun to deviate from the path God originally laid out for us. We do this partly because we don't understand how He created us to be, and partly because we don't know how to apply this in our lives. There is indeed a gap between theory and practice, but we seem to have lost control of both. Even if we come to know God's wisdom and to integrate it into ourselves, that alone is not enough. We must practice God's wisdom in our daily lives.

When our Saviour walked this earth, He asked us to reflect to the world the image of *Christianos*, that is, Christians. *Christianos* means a person in the image and likeness of Christ. To better understand these statements, I want to ask a question using an analogy: What do we get when we squeeze an orange? Obviously, we get orange juice. What do we get when we squeeze a lemon? We get lemon juice.

But what happens when we "squeeze" a faithful Christian? Ideally, we should get what defines their name — the essence of Christ, the essence of the Creator, described as *"gentle and lowly in heart" (Matthew 11:29, NKJV)*. So, let us set out to understand what the art of gentleness means in a selfish world.

"Blessed [makarios]– are the meek, for they shall inherit the earth!" (Matthew 5:5, NKJV). What kind of meekness is being spoken of here? What does the Saviour want to teach us, and what way of life can we discern from this?

The apostle Peter once wrote that a *"gentle and quiet spirit is very precious in the sight of God" (1 Peter 3:4, NKJV).* The question is: What does this meekness refer to, and what do we need to learn in this chamber? Jesus offered Himself as an example. He said: *"Come to Me, all you who labour and are heavy laden, and I will give you rest. Take My yoke upon you and learn from Me, for I am gentle and lowly in heart, and you will find rest for your souls" (Matthew 11:28-29, NKJV).*

Some of us have misunderstood meekness and have disregarded the meek, considering them weak, meaning "soft, dull-witted, slow, or unintelligent" people. In other words, if you can't keep up with others in this society, you are considered inferior. Yet the Bible teaches us to be meek.

―――――•　•――――――

Many believe that being meek is a character weakness in modern man. However, meekness is a voluntary decision to adopt a certain model, a certain type of behaviour.

―――――•　•――――――

Others have come to say that to be meek means "to be docile, easily submissive to anything." Without protest, such a person is obedient, humble, and subservient. Therefore, there is an entire spectrum of opinions regarding this category of people. Yet, there is a clear difference between the meekness they refer to and the meekness our Creator speaks of.

In the expression from Matthew 5:5 (NKJV) *"Blessed are the meek, for they shall inherit the earth,"* we find on the one hand, the description of a person's character and on the other hand, the consequence of meekness. If you are meek, then you are an heir of this earth. The term used in the original writings is the Greek word *praos*, which in Greek culture does not just mean "meek," but also implies the idea of power under control and humility.

Matthew Henry, a theologian known for his biblical commentaries, explains that biblical meekness is not weakness, but an attitude of humility and self-control in the face of challenges[35]. When the Bible was translated into Latin (Vulgate), the term used to translate the Greek *praos* was *mansuetus*, derived from *manu* (hand) and *suetus* (accustomed), thus suggesting a creature that has been tamed or domesticated. This term denotes a disciplined character under control.

These interpretations help us understand that the meekness described in the Bible is a virtue that combines humility with inner strength, thus reflecting the image of Christ in our lives.

---

[35] Henry, Matthew. *Matthew Henry's Commentary on the Whole Bible.* Grand Rapids, MI: Zondervan Publishing House, 1961.

Often, the concept of *"mansuetus"* was used in the context of taming wild animals. In the art of horsemanship, when a Mustang or a purebred stallion is captured, it undergoes a process of taming. A wild horse will not accept a rider on its back; it will struggle, kick, and do everything in its power to resist. After it yields, a radical change occurs: the horse, which previously refused to bear anything on its back, becomes loyal and obedient, showing deep submission to its master, despite being much stronger. Although it has the physical strength to throw off the rider, it submits to its master, accepting that its needs for water, food, safety, and care will be met by this person.

The science that studies the equine family explains that this animal possesses extraordinary intelligence; it understands the mood and sobriety of its master[36]. But why does such a powerful and noble animal submit to its master? Interestingly, God uses a comparison with a wild animal to illustrate the dishonour and lack of loyalty of the people of Israel. In Jeremiah 2, Israel is compared to a wild donkey or *"a wild donkey used to the wilderness, that sniffs at the wind in her desire; in her time of mating, who can turn her away?"* No one will stop her from following her passions: *"All those who seek her will not weary themselves; in her month they will find her"* *(Jeremiah 2:24, NKJV).* This is the opposite of the loyalty and respect that *mansuetus* produces.

---

[36] Hokkaido University. "How do horses read human emotional cues?" *ScienceDaily*, June 21, 2018.

The meekness (*mansuetus*) we are discussing implies the acceptance and habituation to a behaviour or practice that was previously resisted. *Mansuetus* means to subdue someone and make them obedient (in our case, obedient to the Creator).

Here, I want to make a clear distinction between conformist obedience ("I obey you even if I don't agree with you") and obedient submission ("I obey you because I trust entirely in what you say"). God does not want conformists; He desires those who are obedient to His plan. The difference between the two lies in the understanding of dependence on the Creator. While the conformist person obeys out of fear of punishment, the fear of going to hell, the obedient person obeys because they understand and resonate with their master's will.

The meekness (taming) that reflects this principle and leads us to happiness goes through an entire process of mental education, whereby a person learns to become like God.

Now, I want to invite you to analyse a sample of divine mentality that can also become a source of inspiration for us. It is found in a unique combination of ancient texts, often overlooked or read hastily: *"Rejoice greatly, O daughter of Zion! Shout, O daughter of Jerusalem! Behold, your King is coming to you; He is just and having salvation, lowly and riding on a donkey, a colt, the foal of a donkey" (Zechariah 9:9, NKJV).*

To understand the key terms in this text, it is essential to recognise that, although God is the supreme authority, the righteous one, the one who brings salvation with Him, He chooses to be gentle. His behaviour is not tyrannical but full of compassion and leniency towards those around Him. Though He is the only one qualified to be *tzaddok* (the one qualified to bear the sins of the people, the priests), the only one who can offer salvation and decide who will live and who will die, the Creator shows gentleness and compassion towards His own.

When the evangelist Matthew quotes the text from Zechariah 9:9 (NKJV), he inserts something that helps us understand divine pedagogy more clearly: *"Tell the daughter of Zion, 'Behold, your King is coming to you, lowly, and sitting on a donkey, a colt, the foal of a donkey'" (Matthew 21:5, NKJV).* In this text, the terms "righteous," "victorious," and "humble" are replaced with the concept of "gentleness." Thus, biblical gentleness becomes an attitude towards life and a process of character education. Righteousness, the desire to save others, and humility are not innate in man, but are qualities that are learned and cultivated.

The expression "Blessed are the meek" refers to people who allow themselves to be educated and shaped by God. It is *mansuetus* (a taming) at the spiritual level. In other words, it is a process in which we learn to live according to the divine score, not through mere mechanical imitation, but through a deep understanding of divine principles.

This happiness of meekness refers to those who adopt divine ethics and morality by their own will, not by obligation.

Applying this mentality to ourselves, we can say that a meek person is like a noble and powerful animal that chooses to submit to its master out of an unbreakable bond of trust.

Considering the uncomfortable connotation of the term "taming" in the context of human beings, let us explore the divine methodology of character education. Matthew 16:24 (NKJV) tells us: *"If anyone desires to come after Me, let him deny himself, and take up his cross, and follow Me".* This text indicates that following Christ's teachings is a personal choice that comes with no coercion.

In today's society, Christianity has become a global force, but its modern form is often distorted. There is often a dissonance between what is claimed and what is done. The Lord Jesus explained that to follow Him, we must abandon selfishness, accept our cross, and follow the path He has laid out. If we choose to follow Him, we must submit to His process of education, which involves acknowledging our own failures and abandoning inner wickedness. It is essential to understand the role and destiny that God has reserved for us and to take the necessary steps to achieve it. Christianity cannot be reduced to a mere statement of faith; it requires actions that reflect this faith. In short, we must take up our cross and follow Christ.

In his letter to the Ephesians, the apostle Paul explains how we should follow the Lord Jesus, urging us to imitate Him. This imitation is not mechanical but based on observation and comparison, like soldiers who follow the steps of a sapper on a minefield, trusting that he has found a safe path. The Saviour asks us to follow His example, to aspire to become like Him, and to understand why it is vital to be like Him.

To be truly meek, in the sense of praos or mansuetus, we must renounce one of the greatest barriers to character education: pride.

Pride is an exaggerated and unjustified evaluation of one's own worth, through which we consider ourselves superior to others. The Bible urges us to abandon these tendencies to become meek, renouncing not only pride but also arrogance and conceit. Pride is an excessive confidence in one's own abilities, and conceit involves an overestimation of personal skills. Instead, we must embrace humility by recognising our limitations[37].

---

[37] Oxford Handbook of Positive Psychology. "Humility and Interpersonal Relationships." *Oxford Academic*, accessed August 6, 2024. Available at: https://academic.oup.com (Oxford Academic).

How can we be meek people in this world, and how can we anchor our meekness in an ethic that resembles the mentality of our Creator? By understanding the mind of God. *Mansuetus*, at the spiritual level, means accepting and learning the correct ethical and moral code of our Creator, a code we call the Word of God or the Bible. After learning this ethical code, we must apply it correctly in our daily lives.

In the first chapter of this book, we discussed how Psalm 1 begins with the same expression found in Matthew 5: *"Blessed is the man who walks not in the counsel of the ungodly, nor stands in the path of sinners, nor sits in the seat of the scornful; but his delight is in the law of the Lord, and in His law he meditates day and night. He shall be like a tree planted by the rivers of water, that brings forth its fruit in its season [...]" (Psalm 1:1-3, NKJV).* Blessed is the man who has understood the consequences of evil and chooses to remain focused on God's Law. He reads it, understands it, and applies it to his life to produce fruit, which will appear not when he wants it, but at the right time appointed by God.

If you want to be meek and anchor yourself in ethics and morality that align with the will of the Creator, you must accept and correctly apply this ethical and moral code of God in your life. The apostle James clearly tells us: "So then, my beloved brethren, let every man be swift to hear, slow to speak, slow to wrath; for the wrath of man does not produce the righteousness of God. Therefore, lay aside all filthiness and overflow of wickedness, and receive with meekness" — *praotes, mansuetus* (that is, allowing yourself to be taught) — *"the implanted word, which is able to save your souls. But be doers of the word, and not hearers only, deceiving yourselves" (James 1:19-22, NKJV).* How can you be a person anchored in meekness? Receive the Word, learn it, and apply it as God wants.

Spiritually, *mansuetus* means submitting totally to the will of God, putting His instructions into practice in everyday life. Here's an example of obedience to God's will: *"O My Father, if it is possible, let this cup pass from Me; nevertheless, not as I will, but as You will" (Matthew 26:39, NKJV). Mansuetus* is the moment when that Mustang, that purebred stallion, chooses to submit to its master.

What is your relationship with God in the context of character education? Are you open to accepting His will and allowing yourself to be shaped, or are you trying to place conditions on God?

———————● ●———————

It is important not to test God's limits with challenges. He knows what you need before you ask and will provide it at the right time. However, He wants to see if you are willing to bow your will and let yourself be guided, just like a Mustang that allows its rider to direct it.

———————● ●———————

Although you have the power to choose something else and to claim you can succeed without Him, God wants to see that you abandon pride and humbly choose to be obedient to Him. This is the process through which you can educate your character, becoming truly *mansuetus*—gentle and open to the divine will.

"Let nothing be done through selfish ambition or conceit," says the apostle Paul, *"but in lowliness of mind let each esteem others better than himself" (Philippians 2:3, NKJV).* Here, we are talking about an important nuance of the manifestation of *praotes* (the meekness we have already discussed). The term humility, as it is used in Philippians 2:3, is translated from a Greek expression rooted in the concept of *praotes* (meekness). It is not the false humility by which we bow our heads. We humble ourselves not because we are weaker than others, but because we are stronger. We bow not because we are less important than others, but because we have understood our identity as children of God – His princes and princesses – and we want to save our fellow man who is struggling in the agony of sin.

———————• •———————

True values of God do not abuse power. True men and women of God do not abuse their position but are humble and gentle—not in order to impress, but simply because they have learned how to be who they really are, with the help of God.

———————• •———————

They are those who submit to one another in the fear of Christ (Ephesians 5:21, NKJV), because among other things, *mansuetus* means respectful submission to the people of God, in a beautiful pattern where everyone is interested in uplifting others. And what about me? you might ask. It is the role of others to lift you up. And if, in their wickedness, they do not? you might add. Do not fear. God has sworn by His own name that He will repay them.

So how can you be a gentle person?

1. Accept and learn the ethical and moral code of the Creator correctly.

2. Submit your life to the will of God.

3. Submit to the people created by God, to raise them up, and through them, you will also be lifted.

We must understand and accept that people will often set traps for us. When people question your abilities and authority, choose not to treat them with superiority, but with gentleness. At one point, Miriam and Aaron, the siblings of the patriarch Moses, questioned his authority in front of the whole people. Moses was by no means a weak man—he was a prince of Egypt, educated in a culture where he was considered a god. In Egyptian culture, the Pharaoh and his princes were seen as gods, they received the finest education of the time, and they were treated with the highest respect[38].

Therefore, Moses was by no means a soft man, as many believe. When the Bible tells us that Moses was the meekest

---

[38] Magonet, Jonathan. *Numbers: An Introduction and Study Guide: A New Translation with Introduction and Commentary*. Accessed August 6, 2024.

man on the face of the earth (Numbers 12:3, NKJV), it refers to the high standard of his character. He had power, the Spirit of God was within him, and more than that, he had the authority to speak with God as a man speaks to his friend (Exodus 33:11, NKJV; Deuteronomy 34:10, NKJV). At Moses' command, the earth could have opened up beneath Miriam and Aaron. Yet, Moses chose to "negotiate" with God on their behalf. That is what it means to be a gentle person: when people challenge your position, do not respond in kind! Do not think of yourself as superior; rather, lift them up!

In postmodern culture, we are often influenced by social media projections to respond to challenges and criticisms in the wrong way. You have probably heard phrases like, "Who are you to tell me that?"; "Have you taken a look at yourself?"; "Mind your own business!" Nowadays, these responses are often expressed online: we write articles or essays on blogs with the intent to hurt someone, or we post videos in response to what others have shared. However, divine wisdom and mentality do not teach us to act in this way.

An example of gentle behaviour is given to us by David, the man after God's own heart, who did not repay evil with evil. When Abishai, his general, asked why a lowly man named Shimei cursed David (*"Why should this dead dog curse my lord the king? Please, let me go over and take off his head!"* - *2 Samuel 16:9, NKJV*), David replied, *"See how my son who came from my own body seeks my life; how much more now may this Benjamite? Let him alone, and let him curse, for so the Lord has ordered him"* (*2 Samuel 16:11, NKJV*).

When people speak ill of you, let them talk and pray for them. This is how you show that you are a gentle person, that you are *mansuetus* before God. However, if you feel the urge to respond in kind, it means that you are not yet a gentle person. You are still in the second chamber, where you must regret your guilt. Or perhaps you haven't even left the first chamber, where you haven't yet stripped yourself of pride.

You may wonder if it is right to be an army of people who tolerate being hit and slandered without responding. Scripture tells us: *"Bless those who curse you, do good to those who hate you" (Matthew 5:44, NKJV)*, for in doing so, you will win them for God.

Show gentleness when you are hurt.

When the apostle Peter described the Lord Jesus, he said, *"Who committed no sin, nor was deceit found in His mouth; who, when He was reviled, did not revile in return; when He suffered, He did not threaten, but committed Himself to Him who judges righteously" (1 Peter 2:22-23, NKJV)*.

How many of us will not mock when they are mocked? How many of us will not threaten when we are made to suffer? Sadly, very few of us have understood that the meekness that God speaks of – *mansuetus* – means submitting, not to impress, nor to imitate others, but because we understand that only in this way can we take another step toward cultivating divine character and, consequently, toward rediscovering happiness.

You were created to be a chosen one, in the image, likeness, and character of God, not just another inconsequential individual in this world.

You were created to be the light of God in this world. You were created to be His pride, to bear His image and character, and thus to find that state of absolute happiness, hidden deep within you, shackled by the chains of a world that wants to enslave you to its passions.

So far, we have learned that, in order to find the happiness we lost, we must first strip ourselves of our old selves and recognise our personal failure, understanding that we cannot move forward by our own power. We must annihilate pride, arrogance, and conceit and embrace divine humility. We cannot find ourselves as people until we regret wounding our Creator. These regrets will bring healing when we are empathetic—not just sympathetic—toward God, and He will be empathetic towards us. At that moment, when we are stripped of the filthy values of this world and clothed with the desire to follow God, we will have taken the first step toward understanding and learning the art of being gentle people. We will become people who accept being part of the learning process and who apply divine teaching, accepting the divine code projected within us. Then we will shine like the midday sun, and God's smile will be projected over us. His light will clothe us, and all who look at us will see hope, peace, and blessing.

Chapter 7

The Gentle Strength
of Iron Fangs

*"Water boils much faster in small pots
than in large ones."*

This old English proverb highlights the idea that those with narrow or limited thinking tend to react quickly and impulsively, whereas those with broader and deeper understanding remain calm and act with patience.

In this chapter, we will continue to explore the practical elements discovered in the third antechamber, where we learned about the significance of gentleness from a biblical perspective provided by God. We will examine how we can integrate this form of gentleness and wisdom into our daily lives. We aim to cultivate a gentleness that does not merely mean silence or a lack of courage, but rather a proactive attitude, capable of providing the right response at the right moment.

It is essential to do this with nobility and ethics, demonstrating that our gentleness is a manifestation of wisdom. This is controlled tolerance, developed through practice, by embracing the wisdom of our Master, the Creator[39].

The gentleness to which we refer represents the third link in the development of the path toward rediscovering happiness. We cannot be happy unless we decide to start from scratch, understanding that without God, we are nothing, and that gentleness requires education, training, and following the stages mentioned earlier.

In the postmodern collective consciousness, aggressive gentleness, that gentleness of "iron fangs," is a false gentleness that we often encounter around us. It is a form of postmodern cynicism, promoted as the miraculous solution for getting out of difficult situations, but poisonous to oneself and one's relationships. Although people smile politely, you can sense the coldness in their gaze, like hunters waiting to punish you for your mistakes. We must learn to not behave like this, but rather to be lights in this society, so that, upon examining us, those around us see in us an example of divine wisdom to aspire to[40].

Throughout history, the idea of social prescription has been presented to us. We will attempt to understand the causes of this false gentleness, which we often find within ourselves.

Social prescription is a psychological concept that helps us understand how false gentleness functions in the current

---

[39] Foster, Richard J. *Celebration of Discipline: The Path to Spiritual Growth*. HarperOne, 2018.
[40] Peterson, Jordan B. *12 Rules for Life: An Antidote to Chaos*. Random House Canada, 2018.

generation, a generation that has developed to the peak of its capabilities and in which we can no longer find our place. Social prescription is like a formula through which individuals are prescribed specific types of behaviour to follow. In a society where the pace of life is fast and the pressure is constant, people are led in all directions, like ping-pong balls, from one task to another, which makes them stressed and anxious. This continuous pressure leads people to manifest a distorted form of gentleness, which is not authentic but rather an adaptation to external expectations.

Social prescription dictates how we should behave, react, think, and communicate with each other. Instead of cultivating authentic gentleness, we are often forced to display behaviour that aligns with society's norms and expectations, rather than with our own ethics or morality. This hybrid type of gentleness is, in fact, a mask under which frustration and misunderstanding often hide. Social prescriptions can make us lose our authenticity, creating a dissonance between what we truly feel and what we are forced to show[41].

To counteract this tendency, it is essential to reconnect with our authentic values and to develop gentleness from a place of true understanding and compassion. Only in this way can we create authentic and meaningful interpersonal relationships that reflect gentleness emanating from wisdom rather than from the pressure to conform to social expectations.

---

[41] Cialdini, Robert B. *Influence: The Psychology of Persuasion*. Harper Business, 2006.

To understand how we have come to practice hybrid gentleness, let's revisit the two concepts of obedience and conformity, which we discussed in the previous chapter.

In human behaviour, **obedience** refers to the form of social influence exerted by one person over others, involving submission to explicit instructions or commands given by an authority figure. Obedience differs from simple listening because it is a behaviour influenced by the trust we place in others. It is the prescription provided by authority regarding what each of us must do and first requires us to accept that authority, investing our trust in its requirements[42].

There is another form of submission to authority, known as **conformity**. Conformity involves aligning one's behaviour or beliefs with those of the majority, even when internally disagreeing with those decisions. This can lead to an internal conflict where the person outwardly follows the group but does not truly agree with it[43].

A conformist will continue to go along with the group only up to a certain point. As they conform, they may develop feelings of discomfort or dissatisfaction, often described as cognitive dissonance, due to the discrepancy between their true beliefs and their external actions. This internal conflict can accumulate negative emotions, affecting personal wellbeing as the person continues to conform against their own will[44].

---

[42] Milgram, Stanley. *Obedience to Authority: An Experimental View*. Harper Perennial, 2009

[43] Cialdini, Robert B. *Influence: The Psychology of Persuasion*. Harper Business, 2006.

[44] Aronson, Elliot. *The Social Animal*. Worth Publishers, 2011.

It is therefore important for those who aspire to cultivate authentic gentleness—defined here as relating to the world ethically and morally, while being grounded in truth—to become careful observers of their own behaviour and attitudes. They should constantly reflect on whether they are being influenced by external pressures or acting out of respect for ethical and moral principles. By doing so, they can ensure that their actions are guided by integrity and are aligned with the wisdom they seek to embody.

Have you ever wondered why it often seems that you don't fit in with your group of friends? Have you questioned whether you were merely a conformist in that group, inhibiting your tendency to express your opinion for fear of being rejected? In postmodern society, we have often been taught to conform to the majority opinion so as not to offend anyone; in other words, to say what others want to hear and to be tolerant of everyone's ideas.

———————— • ————————

A person who seeks to rediscover happiness, as it is given to us by the Creator, must not declare something they do not agree with.

———————— • ————————

They must learn how to express their personal opinion. At the same time, some say that people who disagree with others are harder to control and harder to tame, like a wild Mustang that is difficult to dominate by the rider's saddle. This conception is mistaken. We must learn how to express our point of view, but to do so with nobility, in an ethical and moral manner. Additionally, we must learn that we will not always have the last word. In this exchange of our states and understanding of our psychological or spiritual condition, we must accept that everyone must participate in the conversation. We must understand that our "opponent" is as noble a person as we are and that if we disagree with their ideas, it does not mean we disagree with them as a person.

We will now analyse several strategic elements related to obedient or conformist listening, considering both the horizontal axis, through which we must view one another, and the vertical axis, through which we must develop a moral and holy character by looking to God. We will see how we can practically apply these elements in our daily life when we feel overwhelmed by life's challenges.

We will now analyse several strategic elements related to obedient or conformist listening, considering both the horizontal axis, through which we must view one another, and the vertical axis, through which we must develop a moral and holy character by looking to God. We will see how we can practically apply these elements in our daily life when we feel overwhelmed by life's challenges.

On the horizontal axis, the gentleness we show to those around us and the way we learn from each other are essential. The Apostle Paul writes a letter to his disciple Timothy, describing the way an authentic believer should be: *"And a servant of the Lord must not quarrel but be gentle to all, able to*

teach, patient, in humility correcting those who are in opposi-
tion, if God perhaps will grant them repentance, so that they
may know the truth" (2 Timothy 2:24-25, NKJV).

Can you imagine a world where people do not argue? Have you ever wondered what it would be like to live in that perfect world where there are no quarrels? The predominant characteristic there is gentleness. Not a feigned, apparent, or manipulative gentleness—rather, one that comes from conviction.

———• •———

If you wish to be part of that ideal world,
you must be prepared to be gracious toward
those who may not yet have reached your
level and correct them gently—not only those
who appreciate you but also your opponents.

———• •———

There is, however, a contrasting peculiarity in our post-modern society. Today, people have learned to be polite and gentle, but in a false way. Though they are ready to attack in their minds, they choose to use irony and sarcasm to keep the situation under control. These behaviours cast a negative and deceitful shadow on their character. They express something entirely different from what they genuinely think. Therefore, if we examine this horizontal axis, a person whose gentleness is a well-educated character trait will do everything in their power to show sincere gentleness in every moment and context[45].

On the vertical axis, gentleness must reflect an authentic relationship with divinity, where the individual aligns their actions and thoughts with divine principles.

———————• •———————

This gentleness is not just an external behaviour, but an internal transformation that takes place when we submit to God's will and shape our lives according to His teachings. Divine gentleness is a manifestation of love and compassion, a way of living that ennobles and enriches the soul.

———————• •———————

The Apostle Peter emphasises the importance of synchronising human character with divine wisdom: *"But sanctify the Lord God in your hearts, and always be ready to give a defence to everyone who asks you a reason for the hope that is in you, with meekness and fear"* (1 Peter 3:15, NKJV). In this verse, the term "meekness" is translated from the Greek word *prautes*, which, as we discussed in the previous chapter, implies the application of benevolent wisdom cultivated through

---

[45] Pluckrose, Helen, and Lindsay, James. *Cynical Theories: How Activist Scholarship Made Everything about Race, Gender, and Identity—and Why This Harms Everybody.* Pitchstone Publishing, 2020.

training and education under God's guidance. Therefore, be a person who responds with gentleness and *"fear [of God], having a good conscience, that when they defame you as evildoers, those who revile your good conduct in Christ may be ashamed"* (1 Peter 3:16, NKJV).

Here, we discern an aspect that acts like a double-edged sword. Some people believe they can be gentle while simultaneously shaming those who speak ill of them. In other words, they train themselves to endure challenges, but their motivation is not constructive, aimed at winning the other over, but rather they seek the opportune moment to bring the other down through their mistakes[46].

We must build a noble character and use gentleness as the holy and moral people do. Our conscience must be clear so that those who gossip about our conduct in Christ will feel ashamed, not before us, but in their own hearts, so that *"in the day of visitation, they may glorify God"* (1 Peter 2:12, NKJV).

Bringing these two axes together, we understand that gentleness must always be expressed in relation to others, while also absorbing the teachings and nobility of the divine character.

Our role is to help others, and our gentleness should be engaged in lifting them up, not in bringing them down. This gentleness must be filled with compassion and empathy.

---

[46] Covey, Stephen R. *The 7 Habits of Highly Effective People: Powerful Lessons in Personal Change*. Free Press, 1989.

Additionally, we must learn to show gentleness even when we are provoked. It is easy to be gentle and calm when everything is quiet and others are too. But problems arise when the storm hits. Regardless of the circumstances around you, try to lift those going through challenges and give them the value they deserve. This is where true gentleness is demonstrated.

However, to become a truly gentle person, you must first pass through the first antechamber—where you shed your ego, pride, and prejudices—and then the second antechamber— where you regret your dominant, critical, proud, and imposing style. If pride begins to dominate gentleness, everything will end in an unstoppable storm. As the proverb says: "Water boils much faster in small pots than in large ones."

To be a "large pot," a character enriched and ennobled by the knowledge of God, you must learn, develop, and practice gentleness.

Gentleness is learned.
Gentleness is developed.
Gentleness is practised.

You might wonder how to be gentle according to the ethical and moral standards of the Creator, that is, according to the Word of God. It is not enough to learn from your fellow human beings; you must access divine teaching, which, over the millennia, has proven infallible. In the third chapter of his epistle, the Apostle James writes that wise and understanding people *"show by good conduct that their works are done in the meekness of wisdom. But if you have bitter envy and self-seeking in your hearts, do not boast and lie against the truth" (James 3:13-14, NKJV).* To possess a gentleness that projects divinity on earth, you must feed on God's mentality and wisdom. Your gentleness must be a projection of wisdom. *"For where envy and self-seeking exist, confusion and every evil thing are there. But the wisdom that is from above is first pure, then peaceable, gentle, willing to yield, full of mercy and good fruits, without partiality and without hypocrisy. Now the fruit of righteousness is sown in peace by those who make peace" (James 3:16-18, NKJV).*

Thus, authentic gentleness is not only a character trait but also a manifestation of divine wisdom. It urges us to act with integrity and live in harmony with God's principles, reflecting His light and love in our relationships with others.

To develop gentleness in accordance with God's wisdom and not with standards created by humans, I invite you to reflect on the following seven principles:

1. Follow an Authentic Model of Divine Gentleness

The best model of gentleness is, of course, the Saviour of the world, Jesus Christ. In his epistle, the Apostle James lists a few benchmarks found in the mentality and practice of the

Saviour, which, once applied, will help you cultivate your gentleness (James 3:17, NKJV).

A gentle person is not interested in defeating their adversaries, but in supporting them and winning them over.

A gentle person is not stubborn but open to change and eager to improve their character and knowledge. Every day, they seek to be better than they were the day before, showing compassion for others. They are not vindictive and do not retaliate against those who have wronged them. Even when they have the opportunity to cause harm, they choose to show mercy and bring comfort to those who have been their enemies. A gentle person bears the fruits of goodness, practising this quality daily.

There is an important difference between doing a good deed and performing an act of kindness. Good deeds can be done by those who merely imitate or try to deceive, but acts of kindness come from true goodness. In the case of acts of kindness, the emphasis is on their source, while good deeds can also be performed by people with bad intentions.

A gentle person does not judge with partiality and does not have two faces: one for themselves and another for others. Gentleness cannot be associated with hypocrisy because it is closely linked to wisdom. We find these qualities in our Creator, who is *"gentle and lowly in heart" (Matthew 11:29, NKJV).* He is easily moved because He has mercy on us, sinners.

Do you remember the thief on the cross who, with his last breath, asked for forgiveness and appealed to the mercy of the Creator, who forgave him with compassion born of empathy, not sympathy? Looking at God, we understand that an empathetic person dedicates themselves to deeply understanding the experiences of those in distress, while sympathy means merely observing from a distance, without real involvement. Empathy means understanding the feelings and causes of another's suffering.

If you want to become a gentle person and to possess the ethical gentleness of the Creator, use this model and learn from Him.

2. Moderate Your Expectations of Others

We are often lenient with our own mistakes and easily forgive ourselves, but when it comes to others, we can have unrealistic expectations. It is important to moderate these expectations and approach relationships with empathy, not just sympathy. Empathy means truly understanding the experiences and emotions of others and recognising that any of us may go through difficult times[47].

Reflecting on the fact that we all share the same human nature and that, as Psalm 103:14 (NKJV) says, we are *"dust and*

---

[47] Brown, Brené. *The Gifts of Imperfection: Let Go of Who You Think You're Supposed to Be and Embrace Who You Are.* Hazelden Publishing, 2010.

ashes," we can develop a deeper understanding of others. This awareness helps us to be gentler and more forgiving because we realise that just as God looks at us with mercy and understanding, we should do the same with our fellow human beings.

When faced with criticism or malice from others, it is essential to remember that they, too, are people who may not yet have reached the same level of understanding or compassion that we are striving to cultivate. Instead of retaliating or defending ourselves harshly, we can choose to respond with gentleness and empathy, thus demonstrating moral superiority.

True greatness does not lie in hurting those who have hurt us, but in lifting up those who have wronged us.

A truly noble person, a person of God, will not seek to tear down but to build, educate, and support. This is the essence of authentic gentleness: to look beyond the bad behaviour of others and see the need for guidance and compassion[48].

Our moral superiority comes from our ability to offer compassion even to those who hurt us, showing empathy for their fallen state. Only a weak person seeks to harm others, while a strong and virtuous person seeks to inspire and uplift. In this way, our gentleness becomes not just an act of kindness, but a

---

[48] Tutu, Desmond, and Tutu, Mpho. *The Book of Forgiving: The Fourfold Path for Healing Ourselves and Our World*. HarperOne, 2014.

manifestation of holiness that draws us closer to divinity and makes us shine in the society in which we live.

3. Invest in the Right Company

To cultivate gentleness and authenticity, it's essential to invest in the right kind of company. The people around you significantly impact your character and values, and surrounding yourself with those who share your moral principles can strengthen these qualities. When you are surrounded by authentic people, you will find support and inspiration to develop your own authenticity. These are people who do not just talk about gentleness but demonstrate it through their actions, being living examples of compassion and empathy[49].

On the other hand, associating with people accustomed to the immoral behaviours of the world can have a corrosive effect on your character. It's like playing with fire; inevitably, you risk getting burned. If you spend time with those who spread negativity and conflict, you will often find yourself in situations that could undermine your integrity and authenticity. In such cases, your gentleness could become nothing more than a mask, deceiving those around you and creating a dissonance between who you are and who you pretend to be.

To prevent this, it's crucial to associate with people who reflect the qualities you wish to cultivate. Seek the company of those who live their lives with true gentleness, showing

---

[49] Maxwell, John C. *The 15 Invaluable Laws of Growth: Live Them and Reach Your Potential.* Center Street, 2012.

empathy and understanding toward others[50]. *"Make no friend-ship with an angry man, and with a furious man do not go, lest you learn his ways and set a snare for your soul"* (Prov-erbs 22:24-25, NKJV). This biblical wisdom highlights the dangers of bad company and stresses the importance of choos-ing your friends wisely.

By learning from the example of those who have demon-strated true gentleness, you will be able to improve your own behaviour. You will thus develop the ability to remain calm in the face of challenges and respond with compassion and integ-rity. In this way, not only will you strengthen your own char-acter, but you will also become a beacon of gentleness and au-thenticity for those around you, inspiring them to follow your example.

4. Do Not Be Quick to Judge

Reflecting on your own mistakes before judging others is essential for cultivating a gentle and forgiving character. Re-membering the times when we made mistakes and were for-given can help us develop empathy and compassion toward others. This exercise in introspection reminds us of the bibli-cal exhortation: *"So then, my beloved brethren, let every man be swift to hear, slow to speak, slow to wrath"* (James 1:19, NKJV). These words encourage us to be attentive and patient, listening before jumping to conclusions.

---

[50] Cloud, Henry, and Townsend, John. *Boundaries: When to Say Yes, How to Say No to Take Control of Your Life.* Zondervan, 1992.

All of us, at some point, have needed the gentleness and understanding of others to overcome our own mistakes. This awareness can help us become those gentle people who are ready to forgive and empathise with others, offering them the same support that we ourselves have received.

* * *

When we find ourselves in a position of power or wisdom that allows us to lift others up, it is crucial to remember our own moments of weakness and error.

* * *

Proverbs 18:17 (NKJV) reminds us that *"The first one to plead his cause seems right, until his neighbour comes and examines him"*. This verse highlights the importance of being open to different perspectives and not relying solely on our own subjective perception. In a complex world, it's vital to align our thinking with divine principles, seeking to filter life's experiences through the mind of Christ. By doing so, we can become true lights in the lives of others, helping them find the path to reconciliation and inner peace.

Therefore, let us always be aware of our own humanity and strive to show the same gentleness and understanding that we desire to receive in return. In doing so, we not only improve our own character but contribute to creating a more empathetic and forgiving society.

5. Cultivate Empathy, Not Sympathy

Cultivating empathy over sympathy is essential for developing a profound and authentic character. Sympathy can offer only a temporary illusion of compassion, keeping us in a state of superficiality. Many people are content to offer sympathy without truly engaging with the emotions and experiences of others, which leads to a lack of depth in their relationships. This superficial approach can dull critical senses and hinder the self-analysis that we need for personal growth[51].

In contrast, empathy means sincerely and deeply connecting with others' feelings and sharing in their joys and sorrows. As we are encouraged in Romans 12:15 (NKJV): *"Rejoice with those who rejoice, and weep with those who weep"*. This level of emotional connection helps us draw closer to others and build authentic, meaningful relationships. Empathy requires a conscious effort to put ourselves in someone else's shoes, to understand their perspectives and emotions, and to respond with sincerity and compassion[52].

To develop this ability, it's important to engage in practices that encourage active listening, careful observation, and self-reflection on how we can truly support those around us. It is a continuous process of learning and reflection that enriches our lives and helps us become beacons of gentleness and

[51] Brown, Brené. *The Gifts of Imperfection: Let Go of Who You Think You're Supposed to Be and Embrace Who You Are.* Hazelden Publishing, 2010.
[52] Neff, Kristin. *Self-Compassion: The Proven Power of Being Kind to Yourself.* William Morrow, 2011.

understanding in our communities. Deepening empathy not only improves interpersonal relationships but also transforms us, making us more aware and responsible for the needs and sufferings of others.

By mastering this art, you can become an example of genuine empathy. In doing so, you will contribute to creating a more compassionate and united world, where every person feels understood and supported.

6. Learn the Lessons from Enemies

When reflecting on the challenges and conflicts with those who are hostile toward us, it is helpful to consider that perhaps our enemies have a role in God's plan, one of teaching us valuable lessons. This perspective allows us to approach conflicts with openness and curiosity, instead of with resentment.

*God can use any circumstance
to develop our character
and strengthen our faith*

Sometimes, the people who challenge or hurt us help us discover aspects of our personality that we might otherwise ignore. These interactions can bring out patience, forgiveness, and gentleness in us, forcing us to surpass our limits and find ways to respond in love and wisdom.

The Bible encourages us to love our enemies and pray for those who persecute us (Matthew 5:44, NKJV). This is not just a call to forgive, but also an invitation to seek deeper meanings and understand the spiritual lessons we can learn from these experiences. When we view every encounter as an opportunity to learn, we open our hearts and minds to personal and spiritual growth.

Instead of responding with anger or revenge, we can choose to see these situations as part of a larger divine plan. This does not mean submitting to injustice or tolerating harmful behaviour, but rather seeking to turn negative experiences into positive lessons that enrich our lives. In this way, our enemies unknowingly become instruments through which God shapes and prepares us for the future.

7. Maintain Focus on Your Purpose

Stay focused and do not allow yourself to be distracted by the constant noise of the world around you. It's easy to lose direction when you are bombarded by external influences that can turn your attention away from your primary goal. In such moments, you may find that the target you are running toward becomes increasingly unclear, while your support system, a vital pillar of your stability, begins to crumble. Without a true point of reference, you will wander among expectations and confusing judgments.

When you lose clarity of purpose, it becomes difficult to moderate your expectations of others. Your company can subtly but significantly change, leading you to make hasty and unfair judgments. Instead of cultivating empathy, you might fall into the trap of superficial sympathy, losing sight of God's true plan for you.

A diverted focus can lead to a series of unwanted consequences, such as confusion and a distorted vision of the path you are following. To prevent these effects, it is essential to keep your focus on your fundamental values and objectives. This focus allows you to maintain your integrity and authenticity amid various external influences.

Remaining faithful to your goals does not just mean ignoring distractions; it also involves developing deep discernment and awareness of the influences that surround you. It is crucial to surround yourself with people who support your vision and inspire you to stay on the chosen path, keeping your eyes fixed on your goals. These people can help you stay motivated and overcome the challenges that arise along the way, providing the necessary support to persevere.

Reflect on your priorities and identify what truly matters. When you do so, you will be able to navigate through the noise of the world with wisdom and clarity, staying firm on your path toward fulfilling God's divine plan for your life.

Chapter 8

— ❧ —

Hungry and Thirsty
for Righteousness

*"Blessed are those who hunger and thirst for
righteousness, for they shall be filled!"
(Matthew 5:6, NKJV)*

We now step into the **fourth antechamber**, where we
will learn that those who hunger and thirst for righteousness
reflect the character of God, and they will be filled with divine
wisdom (Matthew 5:6, NKJV). This is the core of life: those
who hunger and thirst for righteousness are the only ones who
will know true happiness.

Imagine a tree: it has deep, unseen roots, a strong trunk,
and a beautiful crown. The first three antechambers we have
passed through so far represent those hidden roots—the unseen foundation of our spiritual life. In this chapter, we will

focus on the trunk of that tree, which becomes visible and tangible in our daily lives.

To hunger and thirst for righteousness
means to cultivate an attitude that is evident
and distinct to all those around us.

But what does it really mean to be righteous people? According to the dictionary, righteousness is a quality that entails a blameless, sinless, guiltless life—a state of purity and innocence. This is obviously an impossible state to attain by our own efforts. When we honestly examine ourselves, we quickly realise that there is no one in this world who is without sin. Yet, the Word of God tells us that only the righteous are blessed. How can we reconcile these ideas?

The Greek term from which the word "righteousness" is translated is *dikaiosini*. Literally translated, this term does not necessarily mean "blameless" or "sinless," but rather "just" or "justified." A more accurate translation might be: *"Blessed are those who hunger and thirst for justice."*

But what is the connection between righteousness and justice in this context, and what did the translator wish to highlight? If righteousness is a state of moral purity, justice is a principle that demands giving each person what they are due and respecting everyone's rights. To justify means to confer someone the right to something, to authorise, to make them right.

Is there a connection between righteousness and justice? Can someone become righteous merely by following the prescriptions of justice? Or is more required? How do we reconcile this idea with the sacred texts that tell us, *"But how can a man be righteous before God?" (Job 9:2, NKJV)* How could man be justified before God?

The answer to this difficult question is found in the Word of God, in Romans 3:21-24 (NKJV): *"But now the righteousness of God apart from the law is revealed, being witnessed by the Law and the Prophets, even the righteousness of God, through faith in Jesus Christ, to all and on all who believe. For all have sinned and fall short of the glory of God, being justified freely by His grace through the redemption that is in Christ Jesus."*

Why, then, was it necessary for Christ to die on the cross? Why couldn't He just declare the cancellation of man's sin, given that He was the supreme authority? The answer lies in the concept of divine justice. Hebrews 9:22 (NKJV) says, *"Without the shedding of blood, there is no forgiveness."* Violating divine justice would have meant an act of corruption on the part of God Himself. In Christianity, sin is seen as a barrier that separates man from God, and this separation requires reconciliation—a reconciliation carried out according to a strict Law that cannot be ignored.

Christ's sacrifice was not just a symbolic gesture but a demonstration of divine love and justice, showing that sin cannot be overlooked without paying an appropriate price through the shedding of blood, which symbolises cleansing and purification[53]. Christ's death and resurrection are seen as a victory over sin and death, offering the hope of eternal life to those who believe. Righteousness, or justification, cannot be achieved by human efforts; it is a gift given by grace[54] demonstrating God's goodwill, not a total cancellation of the responsibilities of believers.

However, this does not mean that we can rest easy, believing we have nothing more to do in our life of faith simply because we have been granted access to the Creator. To be *"hungry and thirsty"* for righteousness means to seek justice and spiritual purity with the same intensity with which we seek food and water when we are hungry and thirsty. This reminds us that happiness and spiritual fulfilment come from an authentic relationship with God and a commitment to live according to the teachings of Christ.

Proverbs 4:25-27 (NKJV) tells us: *"Let your eyes look straight ahead, and your eyelids look right before you. Ponder the path of your feet and let all your ways be established. Do not turn to the right or the left..."* In other words, do not play with God's laws and do not adapt them to your liking.

---

[53] Stott, John R. W. *The Cross of Christ*. IVP Books, 2006.
[54] Wright, N. T. *Surprised by Hope: Rethinking Heaven, the Resurrection, and the Mission of the Church*. HarperOne, 2008.

Returning to the phrase *"Blessed are those who hunger and thirst for righteousness" (Matthew 5:6, NKJV)*, why did the Saviour choose to speak of justice in terms of hunger and thirst? Hunger and thirst are instinctual needs, essential for our physical survival. In the same way, justice and righteousness should be essential needs for our spiritual survival.

Justice or righteousness cannot be imitated, just as hunger and thirst cannot be faked. They must come from a deep and authentic desire, from an inner spiritual need.

We are human, and we sin every day. How do righteousness and justice align with the sin in our lives? Is the justification we spoke of earlier automatic, regardless of our actions? Or is there still a responsibility to live in accordance with this righteousness?

The answer lies in the connection between justice and truth. Proverbs 3:3 (NKJV) tells us: *"Let not mercy and truth forsake you."* The word "truth" comes from the Hebrew emet, which means "truth." Thus, to be a just person means to live in truth, to remain under the authority of the One who can justify us, make us righteous, and then walk in the light of this truth.

Truth must be demonstrated, not merely declared, because an unsupported statement becomes a lie—either by omission, by misleading, or by distorting reality. We cannot claim to be good people if we cannot demonstrate goodness through concrete actions.

But why is it so important to apply justice in practice? Can't it just remain at the level of declaration? The answer is found in the Law of the Creator: *"But seek first the kingdom of God and His righteousness, and all these things shall be added to you" (Matthew 6:33, NKJV).*

Every law requires a methodology to be applied. Otherwise, the law becomes just an unfulfilled theory, a debated philosophy that will never be put into practice. If justice is the Law of God, then it must be manifested concretely.

Psychology states that any values or beliefs held by a person must be practically demonstrated in order to be considered genuine. They must become attitudes, and these attitudes must transform into behaviours. Without these manifestations, beliefs and values have no consistency[55].

Modern Christianity has become bogged down at this point: we live in times where righteousness and justice are no longer authentically valued. People have become accustomed to the idea that God grants righteousness to all who merely declare they believe. However, we have forgotten that we must share and practise this righteousness, not just claim it through words.

---

[55] Schwartz, Shalom H. "An Overview of the Schwartz Theory of Basic Values." *Online Readings in Psychology and Culture*, vol. 2, no. 1, 2012.

The phrase *"Blessed are those who hunger and thirst for justice" (Matthew 5:6, NKJV)* refers to those who desire justice with the same intensity they would desire food or water when lacking it. This desire must be deep and instinctual, not just superficial or declarative.

For instance, when you pass by an injured person and ignore them, you are not demonstrating justice. When you encounter a sinner and ignore them, you are not demonstrating justice.

———————•—•———————

When your Christianity is merely a repetition of what you have learned from others, without being anchored in the Word of God, you are not demonstrating justice.

———————•—•———————

To be a just person means to live according to the Law of Christ. However, unfortunately, we have become used to justifying ourselves. If Christ has justified us and made us right before God through His blood, we must continue this work by manifesting justice in our daily lives.

Unfortunately, contemporary Christianity has turned into a form of "spiritual banditry" – an attempt to justify one's own mistakes through pseudo-righteousness. For instance, bandits would rob the rich to distribute goods to the poor, believing they were doing justice. However, when it comes to spirituality, we cannot validate righteousness through sin. We cannot claim to justify someone by committing another wrong. For example, we cannot steal to feed someone and then claim we have done justice. Food obtained through sin remains tainted by sin[56].

How did we get here? Because we have legalised a type of self-righteousness which is detached from divine standards. We are no longer hungry and thirsty for God's righteousness, but for a pseudo-righteousness in which man is the measure, not God's Law. We have forgotten that *"Cursed is the man who trusts in man" (Jeremiah 17:5, NKJV)*. This is why the happiness we seek becomes elusive and short-lived. This is why the things that bring us joy today become sources of boredom tomorrow. The happiness of acquiring something, whether it is a new car or a house, is temporary because we no longer evaluate things through the lens of God.

What can be done? How can we correct this error? First of all, righteousness must be received from God, through the sacrifice of Jesus Christ. He paid for our guilt, and we are justified by faith and invited to act upon it.

Do you see that we have a responsibility? Not to cleanse ourselves from sin – this matter was exclusively resolved by the Saviour at Golgotha. In this respect, we have no power: neither to forgive nor to cleanse ourselves of sins. Only Christ can do that. But from that state of cleansing and sanctification, we must manifest God's righteousness in our lives.

---

[56] Lewis, C. S. *Mere Christianity*. HarperOne, 2001.

Can someone who truly understands divine righteousness tolerate sin? Ideally, no one should continue in sin. Yet today's Christianity tends to accept everyone as they are, without making recommendations for change. Any attempt to address sin is met with questions like, "Who are you to judge?" Often, our churches promote superficial happiness, with well-delivered sermons and songs, but we live very little of the values we proclaim. The result is a gap between our beliefs and our actions.

To live according to divine righteousness, we must constantly hunger and thirst for righteousness, actively manifesting it in our daily lives. This is not just a call to faith but also to action.

Although the number of Christians is growing, their impact on the world remains limited. Even in regions with numerous religious organisations, the crime rate has not changed significantly over the years.

This raises an important question: if we are truly hungry and thirsty for righteousness, why don't we have a greater impact on the world around us?

Why are our actions not distinct from those of non-believers? At work, we often tolerate wrong behaviour under the guise of tolerance, instead of living out our authentic faith and upholding divine principles.

We have turned into "spiritual bandits," deluding ourselves that merely attending church is enough. Some live in sin but believe they can compensate for it by financially supporting the church, thinking they are buying righteousness[57]. However, salvation and God's righteousness cannot be bought. God is both loving and just, and righteousness requires an authentic commitment, not opportunism. Opportunism, defined as adopting principles or opinions based on circumstances to satisfy personal interests, cannot replace true faith and righteousness.

As Blaise Pascal[58] said, we often accept ideas because they are presented convincingly, without examining them critically. We must be vigilant about the world's influence on our minds and filter the messages we receive through the lens of divine teachings. True transformation comes from living out our faith, letting our actions reflect our values. Only then can we bring about meaningful change and spiritual fulfilment in the world.

Why have we become opportunists? Because we have redefined how we approach the essentials. We somehow teleported into this "antechamber of righteousness" without passing through the first antechamber, where we strip away the self and let go of pride and prejudice. Perhaps we skipped the second antechamber as well, where we should have learned to regret our mistakes. We've started treating sins as mere errors. Someone once told me that we no longer sin, we just make mistakes. However, God doesn't look at the terms we use to

---

[57] EvanTell. "Authenticity: The Missing Ingredient in Evangelism Today." *EvanTell.org*, 2020
[58] Pascal, Blaise. *Pensées*. Penguin Classics, 1995.

describe our actions but at the wound we create. Our sin produces a wound that hurts just as much, regardless of what we call it: sin, mistake, or error. That wound is aimed against God.

"Whoever says he has not sinned," the Bible teaches us, *"is a liar, and the truth is not in him"* (1 John 2:4, NKJV). We, who have sinned, must remember that we have an *"Advocate with the Father"* (1 John 2:1, NKJV), who has justified us. Yet, justification comes with responsibilities. Christ transforms us, and God sees us as good and righteous, but from this point forward, we must demonstrate these qualities practically in our lives.

Think about when you started a new job. Before becoming an employee of that company, you had no obligations toward it. However, after signing the contract, once you were accepted and employed with legal rights, you also received a series of responsibilities. To be hungry and thirsty for righteousness does not just mean being justified by God to reach heaven. It means that after God has justified and deemed you righteous through Christ's sacrifice, you must practice this righteousness in your daily life.

Are you a righteous person? Are you a person of righteousness? Easy to say, but hard to do. What do you do if you see your best friend stealing? Do you tell him what he did was theft, or do you pretend you didn't see it? If you see your child committing a sin, do you tell them they did something wrong? Or will you, out of parental love, bend God's law? If you choose the latter, you are not hungry for righteousness; you are a "spiritual bandit."

To truly live a life of righteousness and authentic faith, you must draw your strength and inspiration from a divine source. The repentance, peace, and mercy you show must be genuine and reflect fundamental spiritual values. A person of righteousness will complete everything they start, especially in their life of repentance. Theoretical knowledge of the Bible is not enough. If your actions contradict these principles, righteousness remains just an impossible ideal.

In the pursuit of an authentic and meaningful life, we are called to live with integrity and passion for the values that define us.

Though temptations and distractions are constant, our true calling is to anchor ourselves in the principles that enrich our existence. Living according to these values is not just an ideal but a way of life that requires us to take responsibility for our actions and strive to do what is right.

True integrity requires courage and determination. It begins with self-examination and the desire to correct our mistakes. We must constantly ask ourselves whether our actions reflect the principles we stand for. This ongoing pursuit of integrity not only transforms us but also inspires those around us to adopt the same values. Every step we take toward living a just and righteous life adds value and integrity to the community in which we live.

Imagine a world in which every person lives with a commitment to goodness, and in which every decision is made with the common good and moral values in mind. This is the world we can build together, a world where each of us plays a vital role. Righteousness is not just a personal goal, but a collective effort that brings about real change and progress.

May each of us choose to be a beacon of light and integrity in the world, inspiring those around us to follow the same path. Through our commitment to these values, we can transform not only our own lives, but also the communities in which we live, contributing to a better and more just world. Let us be people who not only speak of these values, but who live them and actively promote them, showing those around us the transformative power of authentic principles. In this way, we can enjoy a life full of meaning and contribute to creating a world where every individual has the chance to prosper in the spirit of goodness and truth.

Chapter 9

The Passion of the Righteous

"As the deer pants for the water brooks,
so pants my soul for You, O God.
My soul thirsts for God, for the living God.
When shall I come and appear before God?"
(Psalm 42:1-2, NKJV).

Passion is an intense and deep feeling of enthusiasm or desire for something. It is not just a simple interest or a hobby; it is an internal drive that gives us energy and motivation. The things that truly bring us satisfaction gradually become passions that drive us to live a life full of purpose and meaning[59]. This passion enables us to walk the paths God has prepared for us with a smile on our faces and deep joy in our hearts, as it is written in Psalm 71:23 (NKJV).

---

[59] Dallas Willard, *The Divine Conspiracy: Rediscovering Our Hidden Life in God* (New York: HarperOne, 1998

In this context, passion is not just a fleeting emotion, but an anchor that keeps us firmly rooted in righteousness and truth.

Righteousness and truth are the standards by which those who wish to see God are guided. Like a banner, our passion for righteousness and truth guides us through life's challenges, offering us direction and purpose. In the previous chapter, I was mentioning that the term "righteousness" is synonymous with "justice." In Greek, the word *dikaiosini* means both righteousness and the justification of a person. This connection highlights the importance of living a life in accordance with the principles of justice; and not just in any way, but with a specific attitude: like those who *"hunger and thirst for righteousness, for they shall be filled" (Matthew 5:6, NKJV).*

Hunger and thirst are fundamental needs that sustain human life. They appear instinctively, without a person deciding to be hungry or thirsty. Similarly, the desire for righteousness—the hunger and thirst for uprightness and truth—must be instinctive for the true children of God. It is not merely a conscious choice, but a deep need to live according to divine principles. What kind of hunger and thirst is the Bible speaking about? What needs to change for these desires to become part of our daily lives?

Truly blessed and happy people do not settle for a fleeting experience of righteousness. They are not satisfied just because they have once tasted the abundance of righteousness and been filled. Instead, they feel a constant need to live as righteous, ethical, and moral people. This continual desire motivates them to seek righteousness at every moment of their lives, transforming this search into a way of life that brings spiritual fulfilment and inner peace.

In this chapter, we will explore how to channel the energy accumulated through the process of self-denial, through sincere regret for sin, and through the softening of the heart. We will introduce an essential concept in this context: **spiritual appetite**. Physiologically, hunger and thirst are automatic instincts that sustain life, but appetite is a more complex concept that involves education and controlled exposure to information. Similarly, if physical hunger and thirst are instinctive, hunger and thirst for truth must be an integral part of our spiritual instinct. This implies that the appetite for righteousness and truth must be educated with the same care we use to educate our food preferences. Without proper education, we risk developing a distorted understanding of righteousness, which can become twisted and counterfeit. Such a perspective can lead us to a truth devoid of value, that is filtered through the lens of relativism[60].

---

[60] Joshua Greene, *Moral Tribes: Emotion, Reason, and the Gap Between Us and Them* (New York: Penguin Press, 2013.

If we do not educate this spiritual appetite, we expose our-selves to the danger of functioning according to deformed mor-al standards. Our righteousness can become mutilated, losing its essence and turning into a convenient but false version of what it should be. Thus, we end up following a truth that is no longer authentic and building a fabricated faith. This faith might be permissive towards sin, portraying a God who indis-criminately accepts all our desires and whims.

To prevent this scenario, we must dedicate ourselves to educating our spiritual appetite.

This means constantly exposing ourselves to authentic teachings, seeking wisdom, and cultivating a deep understanding of moral and ethical values.

Only in this way will we be able to live a life anchored in truth and righteousness, a life that truly reflects God's will and leads us to an authentic relationship with Him. In this way, we ensure that our spiritual appetite guides us towards a life of integrity, dedication, and genuine faith.

As mentioned earlier, appetite is an aspect that is educated through a specific diet. According to the *Oxford English Dictionary*, appetite is "a natural desire to satisfy a bodily need, es-pecially for food," and "a strong desire or liking for something."

It is an overwhelming desire, so intense that you feel the need to direct your energy toward a specific goal. On the other hand, diet—a concept we will also use in our analysis—refers to a regimen of food and drink, often implemented for health or therapeutic purposes.

In the same way, a spiritual diet serves to educate our desires and guide our spiritual appetite.

This type of education does not encourage us to seek sin or to support immorality and faulty ethics. On the contrary, it urges us to direct our desires toward God's righteousness, to aspire to His righteousness and truth. When we truly desire His righteousness, God will also provide the other things we need for life[61].

Imagine a vase containing beautiful spring tulips. If we add ink to the crystal-clear water, we will notice that, although the flowers will retain their beauty for a short time, they will gradually begin to take on an artificial colour. This happens because, along with the nourishing water, the flowers also absorb the ink, thus altering their natural shade.

---

[61] James K.A. Smith, You Are What You Love: The Spiritual Power of Habit (Grand Rapids, MI: Brazos Press, 2016

In the same way, the elements we add to our spiritual diet can influence and transform the nature of our beliefs and values. The spiritual diet adopted in a congregation works like the water in the vase, having the power to shape spiritual appetites and change the future behaviours of its members. The way we learn to nourish our souls and quench our thirst, developing a passion for God's righteousness and truth, will become an instinct that shapes our spiritual identity. Thus, the spiritual diet reflects how an entire congregation lives out its Christianity and manifests its faith.

We call ourselves Christians, a term derived from the Latin *christianos*, which refers to those who bear the mark of Christ, identifying with Him not only through teachings but also through their mentality and way of life. Christ, the incarnate God, came to earth to teach us truth and righteousness (John 14:6; 18:37, NKJV).

Christ showed us how to live in truth, not just by knowing it, but by applying His teachings practically, and not just by obeying the Law, but by living it out in everyday life.

In light of this divine example, we must educate ourselves through a spiritual diet and adopt the methods by which we reflect God's righteousness and truth in our lives. In this way, we ensure that we are true bearers of the name Christian, living a life that faithfully reflects the teachings and spirit of Christ.

Is your sense of justice distorted? Is your righteousness something you practice merely to escape hell? Or is it something through which you do *"the good, acceptable, and perfect will of God" (Romans 12:2, NKJV)*, because you've realised that this is the only way you can please your Creator? This is a question each of us must answer. By making God happy, you will also find happiness.

Just like those tulips that draw nourishment from what they are given, you too may start absorbing toxic ink into your spiritual life, if you're not careful about the vase from which you draw your sustenance; you will eventually lose the original beauty that God gave you.

To ensure that we develop a healthy and appropriate spiritual appetite that helps us adopt righteousness and truth as instinctual qualities, we need to implement a correct methodology for mindset education.

In this regard, here are some effective strategies that we will explore in more detail:

1. Leverage the momentum and the strength you gained in the first three antechambers

Draw upon the spiritual energy you've cultivated at the beginning of your journey. The divine insights gained during these foundational phases will serve as vital tools for navigating life with discernment and wisdom.

———————— • •————————

Many people try to mimic righteousness and truth without letting go of their personal pride; they don't realise that true happiness comes from acknowledging their own limitations and their need for God.

———————— • •————————

Without this humility, those led by selfishness will practise a distorted form of righteousness, filtered through pride and prejudice, and often judging others. In contrast, those who embrace humility and accept their limitations will experience authentic spiritual growth. They accept the truth without reshaping it for their own convenience; this places them at odds with the tendency of modern Christianity to proclaim without understanding and promise without practising. These individuals grasp the value of eternity over the fleeting pleasures of the moment.

True repentance for your mistakes is a powerful engine for personal and spiritual transformation. Sincere acknowledgment of guilt isn't just an act of humility, but a sign of spiritual maturity. When we genuinely repent, we show our awareness of our inner truth and our responsibility to both ourselves and others[62].

This genuine repentance must be a transformative force, guiding us down the path of righteousness. As we move forward,

---

[62] Brené Brown, *The Gifts of Imperfection: Let Go of Who You Think You're Supposed to Be and Embrace Who You Are* (Center City: Hazelden Publishing, 2010).

we realise that we are entitled to consider ourselves children of God. Justification comes from sincerely accepting God into our lives and from desiring to live according to His teachings. In this process, we begin to heal the wounds we've caused our Creator and those around us and recognise that these wounds not only affect our relationship with God, but also our relationships within the wider community.

Recognising and accepting this pushes us to allow ourselves to be guided and tamed by God. Just like a powerful animal that recognises its master and bows its head in submission and respect, we too are called to acknowledge divine authority. While we may have the power to impose our will, we consciously choose to let God lead us. This reflects an act of trust and faith, which helps us overcome selfishness and pursue true goodness[63].

When we allow God to guide us, His pure truth begins to shine within us. It is no longer twisted by our selfish desires or by our need to justify our actions, but instead becomes a clear light that guides our steps. Living in this truth, we become living examples of divine love and righteousness, positively impacting our own lives and the lives of those around us.

2. Master the Art of Self-Control

It is crucial to be mindful of daily pleasures and habits that, although legitimate, can consume too much of our time and energy, distracting us from our spiritual priorities. This

---

[63] Rick Warren, *The Purpose Driven Life: What on Earth Am I Here For?* (Grand Rapids: Zondervan, 2002).

includes activities like sports, hobbies, the arts, how we spend our free time, and how we interact with others. While these activities are beneficial in themselves, we must recognise that when we place excessive importance on them or indulge in them at inappropriate times, they can diminish our spiritual appetite and our focus on Christian living[64].

The Apostle Paul illustrates this well in his letter to the Corinthians: *"Now this I do for the gospel's sake, that I may be partaker of it with you. Do you not know that those who run in a race all run, but only one receives the prize? Run in such a way that you may obtain it. And everyone who competes for the prize is temperate in all things. Now they do it to obtain a perishable crown, but we for an imperishable crown. Therefore, I run thus: not with uncertainty. Thus, I fight: not as one who beats the air. But I discipline my body and bring it into subjection, lest, when I have preached to others, I myself should become disqualified (1 Corinthians 9:23-27, NKJV).*

This is the right attitude toward life! Paul understood that channelling our energy, our hunger, and thirst for righteousness in the right way helps us to know God's truth. These instincts must be trained through a good spiritual diet. A healthy diet will cultivate a healthy spiritual appetite. However, we must understand what we are striving for, we must have a clear purpose, and we must use the appropriate means to achieve it.

---

[64] Richard J. Foster, *Celebration of Discipline: The Path to Spiritual Growth* (San Francisco: HarperOne, 1998).

Returning to the teaching of Jesus in Matthew 16:24-25, we see that He said: *"If anyone desires to come after Me, let him deny himself, and take up his cross, and follow Me. For whoever desires to save his life will lose it, but whoever loses his life for My sake will find it."* This represents an essential spiritual strategy. Paul adds a practical perspective, saying: *"Imitate me, just as I also imitate Christ"* (1 Corinthians 11:1, NKJV).

This is a reference to the military concept of following the leader who clears the path through dangerous terrain, like an engineer defusing mines. When we follow Christ step by step, we avoid spiritual dangers. Much like the engineer, Christ creates a safe path for us to navigate life's challenges, and we are called to walk exactly in His footsteps, thus ensuring that we remain on the right track[65].

———————— • • ————————

This is the essence of following Christ: aligning our lives with His example and living by His principles, even when it means giving up temporary comfort for a higher purpose.

———————— • • ————————

Throughout His life, Our Saviour demonstrated the importance of restraint and self-control. He chose to refrain from using His divine power at critical moments, showing the supreme

---

[65] Stuart A. Notholt, *Fields of Fire: An Atlas of Ethnic Conflict* (London: Stuart Notholt Communications, 2008.

model of dedication to the divine will. Similarly, we are called to live by prioritising spiritual values over material ones and by recognising that abstaining from excess helps us stay focused on the path to spiritual happiness and fulfilment[66].

3. Develop Empathy Over Sympathy

Be empathetic towards the needs of others, spreading righteousness through your personal example. Those who live according to the principles of righteousness and truth will be guided by these values as they live their life in this world. They do not ignore problems or "sweep things under the rug," nor do they become aggressive with others. Instead, they practise righteousness with empathy, helping all who have fallen to understand the truth—not just those they personally favour.

Empathy is the ability to understand and feel another person's emotions by putting yourself in their place and by developing a profound connection with their experiences. It involves a genuine desire to help and support in ways that are truly beneficial. On the other hand, sympathy is a feeling of compassion or pity for someone specific, without a deep connection with their experiences. Sympathy keeps you at an observer level, where you will not fully understand the situation[67].

People often tend to show sympathy, thus mistakenly believing they are being empathetic. This confusion stems from the fact that sympathy is often deeply rooted in our own

---

[66] Dietrich Bonhoeffer, *The Cost of Discipleship* (New York: Touchstone, 1995.

[67] Roman Krznaric, *Empathy: Why It Matters, and How to Get It* (New York: TarcherPerigee, 2014).

emotions and preferences. When we sympathise with someone, we are influenced by our subjective feelings towards that person, which may cause us to act out of compassion or pity rather than from a deep understanding of their experiences. Unlike empathy, which requires a genuine connection and the ability to understand the other person's perspective, sympathy can remain superficial and centred on our own emotions and preferences. This carries the risk of misinterpreting the needs and feelings of others and providing support that reflects our own needs more than those of the person in need[68].

Understanding this divine mindset, the Apostle Paul urged his young disciple, Timothy, to *"exercise yourself toward godliness" (1 Timothy 4:7, NKJV).*

Godliness means embodying divine behaviour in our lives, showing empathy and kindness to others, and reflecting God's righteousness and truth.

Moreover, Philippians 2:2 offers another piece of wisdom: *"Fulfil my joy by being like-minded, having the same love, being of one accord, of one mind. Let nothing be done through selfish ambition or conceit, but in lowliness of mind let each*

---

[68] Paul Bloom, *Against Empathy: The Case for Rational Compassion* (New York: Ecco, 2016).

esteem others better than himself. Let each of you look out not only for his own interests, but also for the interests of others. Let this mind be in you which was also in Christ Jesus" (Philippians 2:2-5, NKJV). This mindset teaches us that when we are empathetic and compassionate towards others, righteousness and truth become a sweet fragrance around us. By seeing us as examples to follow, others are inspired to draw closer to God.

The Apostle Peter also encourages us to respond with empathy, even when others speak ill of us or treat us as wrongdoers:

Having your conduct honourable among the Gentiles, that when they speak against you as evildoers, they may, by your good works which they observe, glorify God in the day of visitation (1 Peter 2:12, NKJV).

Here we see how the focus shifts from ourselves to God. Our goal is to act in such a way that honour and praise go to Him, and His goodness draws people toward Him.

Understand the needs and struggles of others with empathy and help them see the truth through your example. Be a representative of truth and righteousness in all areas of your life—at work, at school, on the street, with friends, and even in church. When you see others speaking harshly or unjustly about someone, be the one to bring balance and fairness. In places where lies may seem normal, let your actions reflect the truth without fear of losing privileges, because God will fight for you.

Be a person of righteousness not only among believers, but also among those who face difficulties and darkness. Spread the sweet aroma of the Creator and the hope of His divine righteousness. Wherever you go, let God's presence shine through you, bringing peace and hope. Let the people around you see His smile reflected in your life. This is your power to influence the world.

4. Use Your Personal Experiences as Motivation for Others

Whether joyful or challenging, our experiences can serve as sources of inspiration for others. Think of them as life stories that can help people draw closer to God. By adopting divine mindsets and values, these experiences naturally become part of how we live and act daily.

Jesus said, *"As the living Father sent Me, and I live because of the Father, so he who feeds on Me will live because of Me" (John 6:57, NKJV)*. This analogy highlights how integrating the teachings and values of Jesus into our lives can give us purpose and direction. He continues: *"This is the bread which came down from heaven—not as your fathers ate the manna, and are dead. He who eats this bread will live forever" (John 6:58, NKJV)*. This example illustrates that, just as physical food is absorbed and provides energy, spiritual values must be integrated into our souls.

From a psychological perspective, this process resembles how we learn and internalise cultural values. As we absorb these values, they become part of our identity, guiding our actions and decisions.

———————• •———————

By using our personal experiences—
be they moments of joy or trial—
as sources of motivation for growth and
development, we can positively impact
both our own lives and
the lives of those around us.

———————• •———————

This process is not about mechanically imitating what we have seen, but about genuinely integrating these values into our daily lives. The assimilation of spiritual values is similar to how our bodies transform food into energy and vitality[69].

As we integrate these values, we become sources of inspiration and positive change, influencing our communities through our personal example. Thus, our stories become testimonies of ethical and moral principles, which, in turn, helps create a better and more empathetic society.

---

[69] Brené Brown, *Daring Greatly: How the Courage to Be Vulnerable Transforms the Way We Live, Love, Parent, and Lead* (New York: Gotham Books, 2012).

5. Trust and Follow Through the Process of Sanctification

Sanctification is a lifelong journey of personal growth and transformation; it doesn't happen overnight but unfolds gradually as we evolve.

From a psychological perspective, this process involves embracing and integrating new values and behaviours that align with specific moral and ethical principles. Personal transformation includes recognising and abandoning old habits, while embracing and assimilating new values and behaviours. This process mirrors the concepts of personal development in psychology, such as self-reflection and continuous growth. Psychological theories stress that lasting change takes time and dedication, underpinned by a clear set of values and objectives[70]. In the biblical context, the Apostle Paul exhorts us: *"And do not be conformed to this world, but be transformed by the renewing of your mind" (Romans 12:2, NKJV).*

The integration of spiritual values involves becoming aware of our emotions and actions and aligning them with the fundamental biblical principles. In this regard, the Bible encourages us: *"For those who live according to the flesh set their minds*

---

[70] James Clear, *Atomic Habits: An Easy & Proven Way to Build Good Habits & Break Bad Ones* (New York: Avery, 2018).

on the things of the flesh, but those who live according to the Spirit, the things of the Spirit" (Romans 8:5, NKJV).

Cognitive-behavioural psychology studies show that individuals can alter their thought and behaviour patterns through deliberate practices and through adopting a growth-oriented mindset. Here are a few specific mechanisms:

- **Self-reflection and Self-awareness**: It's essential to know ourselves and to understand our emotions and motivations. Through self-reflection, we can identify our strengths and weaknesses, which enables us to work toward continuous spiritual growth. Proverbs teaches us: *"Keep your heart with all diligence, for out of it spring the issues of life" (Proverbs 4:23, NKJV).*

- **Cultivating a Desire for Positive Values**: Just as we develop tastes and preferences in daily life, we can also nurture a desire for biblical values like righteousness and truth. This process involves the conscious choice of influences and resources that contribute to our spiritual growth. As it is written: *"Blessed are those who hunger and thirst for righteousness, for they shall be filled" (Matthew 5:6, NKJV).*

- **Avoiding Negative Influences**: It's important to recognise and avoid the elements that could negatively affect our personal growth, just like we would avoid unhealthy foods in a physical diet. The Bible is clear in its counsel: *"Abstain from every form of evil" (1 Thessalonians 5:22, NKJV).*

As we integrate these values into our lives, we will experience greater satisfaction and personal fulfilment. Studies show that living in alignment with one's values is associated with increased wellbeing and a more meaningful life[71]. Similarly, the Bible reminds us: *"But seek first the kingdom of God and His righteousness, and all these things shall be added to you"* *(Matthew 6:33, NKJV).*

In this context, sanctification can be seen as a practice of self-improvement and continuous growth, which is supported by constant reflection and a commitment to our spiritual development. Not only does this enrich the individual's life, but it also contributes to a better society by promoting righteousness and truth.

Use the teachings you've received to abstain from daily pleasures that may distract you and to focus on what is truly important. Be empathetic toward others and seek to spread righteousness through your personal example. Trust in God throughout this process of sanctification, and you will find true happiness and fulfilment.

---

[71] Jonathan Haidt, *The Happiness Hypothesis: Finding Modern Truth in Ancient Wisdom* (New York: Basic Books, 2006).

Chapter 10

<hr>

Compassion, Mercy and Kindness

"Blessed are the merciful,
for they shall obtain mercy"
(Matthew 5:7, NKJV).

As we have learned in the previous chapters, God created us to be joyful people, who are nourished by His goodness and through His goodness. Yet, we have allowed ourselves to be seduced by the world's philosophies and temptations, becoming trapped in self-centeredness and segregated in a society that seems to have lost its values. This society no longer has a clear purpose, nor a strategy to create communities of happy people.

The Apostle Paul understood that the secret to an authentic and happy life lies in the voluntary manifestation of a divine character, not just in its declaration—sometimes pompous, sometimes mechanical—in a world where clichés are elevated to the rank of virtue. *"Do not be overcome by evil, but over-come evil with good." (Romans 12:21, NKJV).*

We shall continue our journey of searching for our lost happiness and we will pause for a while in the fifth antechamber, where we will learn what divine character means and how we can project it into our lives. Above the door of this antechamber, the words are written in bold: *"Blessed (makarios) are the merciful, for they shall obtain mercy." (Matthew 5:7, NKJV).*

At one point, when the Lord Jesus was questioned by the Pharisees, the Scribes, and teachers of the Law about the way He engaged too closely with people, He responded, *"Go and learn what this means: 'I desire mercy and not sacrifice.' For I did not come to call the righteous, but sinners, to repentance." (Matthew 9:13, NKJV).* In this phrase, Jesus uses the Greek concept of eleos to describe mercy, a term which, upon closer analysis, is better translated as compassion.

The text Christ quotes is found in Hosea 6:6 (NKJV), and it is slightly different: *"For I desire mercy, not sacrifice, and the knowledge of God more than burnt offerings."* Here, we see Hosea using the concept of kindness, while also emphasising the need for a deep knowledge of God, not merely an imitation of Him. Unfortunately, many of us have come to imitate faith and to believe that this is enough to access God's Kingdom.

Why did Christ choose to use this wording instead of presenting the text in its original form? It must be noted that Jesus did not alter Hosea's text; He used the Greek translation of the Old Testament (the Septuagint), which was common and accepted at that time. This is not an intentional change in meaning but reflects the translation differences between Hebrew and Greek. When comparing the two texts, we see how the compassion (*eleos*) mentioned by the Savior aligns perfectly with the millennia-old declaration of the Jewish prophets, who understood that compassion was an expression of goodness. In Hebrew, the concept of *hesed* used by Hosea means an extreme goodness, which stems from kindness, not from imitation meant to impress or win the sympathy of others. *Hesed* includes loyalty, devotion, and steadfast love, all derived from kindness—a concept we have unintentionally oversimplified[72].

Kindness differs from mere good deeds. When we speak of kindness, we refer to a fundamental trait of human character, which later generates acts of kindness.

The emphasis is on the source from which the action flows; that source is kindness. A good deed, however, is the act itself, which can be expressed even by someone with malicious intentions, in an attempt to deceive or manipulate[73].

This is precisely why, when questioned by His adversaries, the Savior sent them to learn what is written in Hosea, specifically referring to *eleos*—compassion. Kindness must be united

---

[72] Karen Nelson, *Ḥesed and the New Testament: An Intertextual Categorization Study*, (Wipf and Stock Publishers, 2012).

[73] Timothy Keller, *Generous Justice: How God's Grace Makes Us Just*, (Penguin Books, 2010).

with compassion. Without compassion, without seeing the other person as worthy of our sacrifice, we cannot be happy. Thus, mercy becomes the first fruit of an authentic believer.

Mercy is not just about understanding the suffering of others; it involves a great deal of empathy. If empathy leads us to sacrifice for others, internalising their suffering, sympathy involves us more for our own sake. Unlike empathy, which is purely altruistic, sympathy contains shades of selfishness.

"I desire mercy," not sympathy, said the Savior of the world. The reason for our spiritual decline is that we have surrounded ourselves with people who offer sympathy but lack empathy.

As you read these lines, you may realise that you too are often lacking in empathy, disguising desires for self-importance, selfishness, and pride under the mask of sympathy.

Compassion is not something we are born with, nor something that can be imitated. It must be filtered through education, understanding, and ultimately, acceptance. Until we accept that we must be empathetic and have compassion for our fellow human beings, we cannot progress on the path to redis-covering happiness[74].

In the Gospel of Luke, chapter 10 (NKJV), Jesus Christ is once again confronted by the Pharisees and the Scribes who tried to trick Him, using His own words. They did not do this because they didn't understand what He was saying, but because they came from a culture of imitation. They lived under the appearance of following the Law, but it was a mechanical adherence: *"Teacher, what shall I do to inherit eternal life?" (Luke 10:25, NKJV)* one of them asked. Essentially, what should I do to be happy? Jesus answered him, *"What is written in the law? What is your reading of it?" (Luke 10:26, NKJV).*

This question reveals one of the great problems of the modern world: how we read and interpret laws. If you have a skilled lawyer who knows how to interpret the law, you can escape punishment, even if you are guilty.

How many of us today read the Law to justify our dirty lives? How many of us flip through the Bible just to find verses that support our sinful behaviour? How many of us exploit the sacred text to obtain a pseudo-happiness that will never be enough?

---

[74] Andrew Peterson, *Compassion and Education: Cultivating Compassionate Children, Schools, and Communities*, Palgrave Macmillan, 2017.

In a way, the teacher of the Law in the parable told in the Gospel represents each one of us. He responded: *"You shall love the Lord your God with all your heart, with all your soul, with all your strength, and with all your mind, and your neighbour as yourself."* To which Jesus said: *"You have answered rightly; do this and you will live." (Luke 10:27-28, NKJV).*

The Savior emphasises here that although we know what we must do, we often fail to put into practice that which we know. Mercy and compassion are not just declarations or intentions. Sympathy can be reduced to mere words, but mercy and empathy are expressed through actions. When you are empathetic, there is no need to say much; what matters is doing what is right. In contrast, when you act only out of sympathy, you are more likely to use words to impress, but actions will be lacking.

The biblical text goes on to say that in his attempt to justify his lack of action—justifications that he believed were supported by the Law— the teacher of the Law asked: *"And who is my neighbour?" (Luke 10:29, NKJV).* This is a question that we, too, often ask. We believe that certain people do not deserve our mercy simply because they have been labelled as sinners or because they have made significant mistakes. We think they should be punished, not forgiven, and that we are certainly not the ones who should show them mercy.

In the parable of the Good Samaritan, Christ teaches us that our neighbour is not just the one close to us in ethnicity or religion, but anyone in need of our help. The mercy and compassion we show to others are the true measures of our faith.

"*A certain man went down from Jerusalem to Jericho, and fell among thieves, who stripped him of his clothing, wounded him, and departed, leaving him half dead. Now by chance a certain priest came down that road. And when he saw him, he passed by on the other side. Likewise, a Levite, when he arrived at the place, came and looked, and passed by on the other side. But a certain Samaritan, as he journeyed, came where he was. And when he saw him, he had compassion. So he went to him and bandaged his wounds, pouring on oil and wine; and he set him on his own animal, brought him to an inn, and took care of him.*" [...] "*Which of these three do you think was neighbour to him who fell among the thieves?*" *And he said, 'He who showed mercy on him.' Then Jesus said to him, 'Go and do likewise.'*" (Luke 10:30-37, NKJV).

Through this parable, Christ highlights that being someone's neighbour means acting with kindness and compassion, regardless of who that person is.

———————•———————

He shows us that mercy must be offered without discrimination and that true justice does not consist only of knowing the law, but in applying it through acts of kindness and compassion.

———————•———————

The justice given by Christ is a call to live a life of mercy and love towards all people, not just those who are close to us or those we like.

So, who is your neighbour? It is the one who needs your mercy, not the one who brings your sympathy to life.

To understand these aspects more clearly, it is important to carefully consider the parable of the Good Samaritan. To a superficial observer, it might seem like just a story meant to stir public emotion. However, at a closer look, this parable reveals subtle details about the mentality Christ sought to dismantle in front of the teacher of the Law, removing every legalistic excuse for not showing mercy or compassion. The priest and the Levite had all the legal arguments on their side not to touch the wounded man. The Mosaic Law clearly specified in Leviticus 15:2-7 (NKJV) the rules concerning the uncleanness of a man due to bodily discharge. According to the Law, touching such a man would have rendered the person who touched him unclean until evening.

Moreover, Leviticus 21:1-4 (NKJV) specified that priests and Levites were not to touch a dead person, except for close relatives. Violating this rule would have resulted in temporary exclusion from service and required undergoing a complex purification process. It seemed that the priest and the Levite had good reasons not to approach the severely injured man, whom they might have considered dead.

───────● ●───────

However, the message of the parable is that mercy and compassion must transcend legal and cultural barriers.

True faith is manifested through acts of unconditional kindness.

Empathy compels us to feel person's pain, regardless of the law or cultural norms. The Samaritan, who had no obligation to help a Jew, was the one who overcame these barriers to show compassion[75].

How would you react if you were in the priest's or Levite's place? Would you risk your reputation, your privileges or your social standing to help someone in need?

Empathy goes beyond legal barriers because you feel the other person's pain. Empathy happens when your heart hurts for someone else, just as a parent feels their child's pain when the child suffers. This is empathy: bearing through the pain alongside your neighbour.

Christ uses the concept of mercy (compassion) in Matthew 5:7 (NKJV): *"Blessed are the merciful, for they shall obtain mercy."* This emphasises the importance of mercy as a primary expression of God's character.

Mercy is not just an occasional action, but a fundamental trait of the divine character.

---

[75] David A. Fiensy, *Hear Today: Compassion and Grace in the Parables of Jesus*, ACU Press & Leafwood Publishers, 2020.

Mercy is thus the central expression of God's character, rooted in His profound nature and in the continuous manifestation of **goodness** and **compassion** towards His creation. *The Oxford English Dictionary* defines *character* as "the mental and moral qualities distinctive to an individual," while mercy is described as "compassion or forgiveness shown towards someone you could punish or harm." Additionally, *goodness* is defined as "the quality of being morally good or virtuous," and *compassion* as "sympathetic pity and concern for the sufferings or misfortunes of others." These traits are reflected in a person's **behaviour**, in their ideas and actions, which, in fact, form the root from which all our deeds spring.

━━━━━● ●━━━━━

If you want to know your character, you only need to analyse your behaviour, your words, and your actions. What you do is your true character, not what you declare about yourself[76].

━━━━━● ●━━━━━

The same is true of God. His character is revealed through His deeds and attitudes, and the Bible shows us that the Lord is merciful and full of compassion and kindness. *"The Lord is merciful and gracious, slow to anger, and abounding in mercy" (Psalm 103:8, NKJV).* This kindness is reflected in the

---

[76] David Brooks, *The Road to Character*, Random House, 2015.

mercy and grace that God shows to all humanity, as an expression of His divine character.

The clearest example of God's merciful and compassionate character can be found in the story of Moses, the Hebrew child who, through providential circumstances, was adopted into the royal family of Egypt, the dominant empire of the time. Saved from the waters of the Nile, Moses became a prince of Egypt and grew up in Pharaoh's household, where both Pharaoh and his sons were considered divine beings. Moses was thus regarded as a deity, before whom people had to bow, either out of conviction or obligation[77].

Nevertheless, God orchestrated history in such a way that Moses would meet, at the appointed time, the true King and God, Yahweh of the Hebrews. In Exodus 33:13 (NKJV), Moses makes a profound request of God: *"Now therefore, I pray, if I have found grace in Your sight, show me now Your way."* The Hebrew term derec used here refers to the way God thinks and acts, to His mindset expressed in deeds.

This request comes at a critical moment. God had asked Moses to lead the people of Israel out of Egypt, but at their first grave transgression, He intended to destroy them all and make Moses the father of a great new nation. Faced with this apparent shift in divine plans, Moses begins to wonder about the nature of God's justice. Was this a God who could so easily abandon the promises made to Abraham, Isaac, and Jacob (Genesis

---

[77] Margaret Maitland, *Pharaoh: King of Egypt*, British Museum Press, 2012.

12:2, NKJV)? In his deep desire to understand the essence of God, Moses asks, *"Show me Your way [...] that I may know You and that I may find grace in Your sight. And consider that this nation is Your people." (Exodus 33:13, NKJV).*

In this dialogue, we see how Moses' character traits begin to emerge. Although he could have accepted the divine offer and become the pillar of a new Israel, he refused, demonstrating compassion for his people. Moses begins to negotiate with God, seeking to save the people of Israel instead of pursuing his own interest[78].

Moses, raised in an Egyptian culture centred on the justice of the law, now desires to understand the justice of a God who seems to change His mind at the first major mistake. In his desire to know the essence of God, he asks, *"Please, show me Your glory!" (Exodus 33:18, NKJV).* The Hebrew term kabod, meaning "weight," refers to something that gives importance and authority. Moses wanted to understand what gave God His distinctive honour and splendour.

In His response, God says to Moses, *"I will make all My goodness pass before you, and I will proclaim the name of the Lord before you. I will be gracious to whom I will be gracious, and I will have compassion on whom I will have compassion." (Exodus 33:19, NKJV).* The term *tuvi*, derived from tov, refers to God's goodness and beauty. In ancient Hebrew culture, tov did not only signify moral goodness but also beauty, generosity, and joy—attributes we perceive when we look at a person.

---

[78] James M. Boice, *The Life of Moses: God's First Deliverer of Israel*, Reformation Heritage Books, 2018.

We see here that goodness is closely linked to beauty, joy, and wellbeing. This is how God manifests His character—by harmoniously uniting all these traits.

Goodness and divine mercy always generate beauty, joy, and happiness.

God promises Moses that He will show him these traits: *"Here is a place by Me, and you shall stand on the rock. So it shall be, while My glory passes by, that I will put you in the cleft of the rock, and will cover you with My hand while I pass by. Then I will take away My hand, and you shall see My back; but My face shall not be seen." (Exodus 33:21-23, NKJV), "for no man shall see Me, and live." (Exodus 33:20, NKJV).*

In Exodus 34:6 (NKJV), we are told how the Lord passed before Moses and proclaimed: *"The Lord, the Lord God, merciful and gracious, longsuffering, and abounding in goodness and truth."* This declaration emphasises the empathetic nature of God. He does not merely express sympathy, but deeply feels the pain, suffering, and hardship of those who have fallen. God draws near to those in suffering, even though He is the Supreme Divinity and man is but dust and ashes.

Furthermore, God adds, *"abounding in goodness (hesed in Hebrew) and truth (emet)."* We see that God changes the perspective and uses the term *hesed*—which represents a deep kindness, the source from which all good deeds flow, including beauty, happiness, and joy. In addition, He emphasises that His goodness is accompanied by faithfulness, expressed through the term *emet*, which means truth.

> ***Thus, divine goodness***
> ***is always clothed in truth***
> ***and projects a joyful and***
> ***happy being.***

Returning to the idea from which we started—mercy—we now understand that its root is found in the character of God. By contrast, sympathy stems from a selfish perspective, attempting to project a false image of what we are not. Genuine mercy comes from a heart filled with kindness, shaped after the divine model, and not from a false smile meant only to impress.

To be merciful is to learn and practise empathy, as the Lord Jesus urged us to do *(Matthew 9:13)*. Through empathy, we open the doors to divine blessings and become magnets for God's mercy.

Mercy is God's calling for each of us, inviting us to reflect divine goodness in concrete deeds. If we do not get actively involved, we remain stuck at the level of unfulfilled words. God shows us what goodness is and what He requires of us: *"To do justly, to love mercy, and to walk humbly with your God."* *(Micah 6:8, NKJV).* He calls us to be like Him, spreading goodness without discrimination, sacrificing not for rewards, but because this is the fundamental trait of His children. As *Matthew 6:33 (NKJV)* teaches us: *"But seek first the kingdom of God and His righteousness, and all these things shall be added to you."* To be truly human means to reflect divine goodness in everything we do.

How can we practise mercy? Scripture offers us clear guidance: *"Let love be without hypocrisy. Abhor what is evil. Cling to what is good. Be kindly affectionate to one another with brotherly love, in honour giving preference to one another."* *(Romans 12:9-10, NKJV).* Brotherly love requires that you value someone else more than yourself and see them as an extension of your own being.

Be a person of kindness, manifesting the divine character of God in the world. These concepts are not always easy to explain or understand, but together we can change the world. We can bring about a reform in Christianity, restoring "salt and flavour" to the world and becoming lights in the darkness.

In this chapter, we have learned that happiness is a reflection of goodness and that it is manifested through mercy and compassion. Kindness is the source from which all pleasant aspects of life flow, and to find true happiness, we must adopt this divine character. Let us therefore become people of kindness and compassion shown towards those around us.

As we continue this spiritual journey, we will explore practical ways to integrate compassion into our lives. We will learn how to manifest divine mercy and kindness in every aspect of our existence. Let us be guided by God's call to become instruments of kindness and compassion in the world, transforming not only our lives but also the lives of those around us. Let us be beacons of light that shine in the darkness, bringing hope and change through our acts of kindness.

Chapter 11

The Practice of Authentic Compassion

In this chapter, we will explore how we can show mercy and empathy, how to deeply connect with the experiences of others, and how to offer them the support they need to stand strong again. By understanding the pain of others, we can respond to them in ways that help them regain their strength and happiness. This, in essence, is compassion.

We begin with a key text: *"He has shown you, O man, what is good; And what does the Lord require of you but to do justly, to love mercy, and to walk humbly with your God?"* *(Micah 6:8, NKJV)*. God calls us to reflect His image in the world, extending forgiveness, empathy, and support to those who have stumbled.

Once a fierce persecutor of early Christians, the Apostle Paul underwent a radical transformation after his encounter with the Saviour on the road to Damascus. He came to understand that God is love and He desires for us to manifest His divine character in the world. After grasping God's will, Paul passed on an essential teaching for all those seeking happiness: *"And be kind to one another, tender-hearted, forgiving one another, even as God in Christ forgave you" (Ephesians 4:32, NKJV).*

Before diving deeper into this topic, it's important to clarify the subtle but crucial difference between empathy and compassion. As we've learned, empathy is the ability to understand and feel what another person is going through—to put yourself in their shoes and feel their emotions. Compassion, however, takes it one step further. It not only involves understanding their suffering but also includes a genuine desire to help and alleviate that pain. Compassion is, therefore, an active form of empathy, expressed through concrete actions that aim to reduce or eliminate someone else's suffering[79] [80].

God calls us to be empathetic in every situation: *"Rejoice with those who rejoice, and weep with those who weep. Be of the same mind toward one another" (Romans 12:15-16, NKJV).*

We will explore below some essential aspects to recalibrate our mindset so we can rediscover happiness and practise compassion authentically and wholeheartedly, without turning it into an imitation that is superficial or self-serving.

---

[79] Paul Gilbert, *The Compassionate Mind* (London: Constable & Robinson, 2009), pp. 15-17.
[80] Kristin Neff, *Self-Compassion: The Proven Power of Being Kind to Yourself* (New York: William Morrow, 2011), pp. 10-12.

Mercy and compassion are fundamental concepts, but they are often misunderstood in contemporary society. In a world that is increasingly digital and fragmented, empathy feels like a lofty ideal that is difficult to reach. Influenced by technology and the fast pace of modern life, the current generation has transformed empathy into something complex and confusing. We live in a society where hatred and social comparisons divide us. We filter our reality through a digital lens, presenting idealised versions of our lives to meet societal expectations.

This phenomenon has led to deep isolation, where people feel utterly alone in real life, even though they are surrounded by numerous virtual friends. Social media creates an illusion of connection, but in reality, relationships have become shallow and impersonal. Thus, we find ourselves alone in the midst of a crowd of virtual companions[81].

In this context, empathy and compassion become essential tools to rebuild authentic human connections. Communicating through screens and text messages makes it harder to truly understand the emotions and needs of others, which contributes to the dehumanisation of relationships and leading to transactional, surface-level interactions.

Compassion isn't just an abstract concept; it's a central part of Christian teaching. Jesus Christ placed empathy at the heart of His message: *"A new commandment I give*

---

[81] Sherry Turkle, *Reclaiming Conversation: The Power of Talk in a Digital Age* (New York: Penguin Press, 2015), 21-25

to you, that you love one another; as I have loved you, that you also love one another. By this all will know that you are My disciples, if you have love for one another" (John 13:34-35, NKJV). This commandment highlights the importance of empathy in Christian life and in our relationships with others.

Empathy is one of the fundamental traits of God's character, a trait He also placed within us when He created us in His image and likeness.

Mercy must be shown responsibly, not just as a religious duty, but as a way of living in harmony with divine values. It's important to ask ourselves whether our attempts to help others are motivated by genuine empathy or simply by superficial sympathy. True empathy involves self-sacrifice and the projection of our love onto others.

One of the most precious gifts God has given us is the ability to be empathetic. This means to emotionally identify with the feelings and experiences of others. The Apostle Paul emphasised the importance of this when he said: *"It is more blessed to give than to receive" (Acts 20:35, NKJV),* pointing out that true happiness comes from self-sacrifice, not from accumulation.

In the form of self-sacrifice, love is essential for empathy. To project our love onto others means to identify with their pain and needs, not out of moral duty, but from a deep understanding of their suffering. Empathy is a sign of our belonging to the body of Christ and to His Church. It is a divine standard, and without it, we cannot find true happiness.

The Lord Jesus Christ left us a clear and comprehensive commandment: *"You shall love the Lord your God with all your heart, with all your soul, with all your mind, and with all your strength"* and *"You shall love your neighbour as yourself"* (Mark 12:31, NKJV). In our relationship with God and with others, everything must be filtered through the lens of self-sacrifice. This synergy of the body works for the good of the whole, not for individual gain.

———• •———

Conflicts are inevitable in our relationships. In such moments, empathy must be accompanied by forgiveness, and that forgiveness must be complete.

———• •———

Mark Twain once said, "Forgiveness is the fragrance that the violet sheds on the heel that has crushed it." Forgiveness releases us from bitterness and allows us to be truly empathetic. Don't hold grudges, as they will only chain you to suffering, as theologian R.T. Kendall explains in his book *Total Forgiveness*. After a conversation with Pastor Iosif Țon, Kendall learned that as long as he remained stuck in bitterness, he was imprisoned by it. Taking this advice, Kendall reconciled with Martin Lloyd-Jones, right when Lloyd-Jones was on his deathbed. This last-minute reconciliation saved both men from great emotional suffering[82].

---

[82] R.T. Kendall, *Total Forgiveness*, Revised and Updated Edition, Charisma House, 2007.

Forgiveness is essential for compassion. The Apostle Paul urges us: *"Do not be overcome by evil, but overcome evil with good" (Romans 12:21, NKJV)*. If you want to be a person of empathy, you must be ready to forgive. You might ask: How can I forgive?

Although forgiveness isn't always easy, it is a divine gift that helps us live a life free of resentment. God has already created us with the capacity to forgive, and this mechanism exists within us. To activate it, we need to reflect on biblical teachings such as those in Ephesians 4:32: *"And be kind to one another, tenderhearted, forgiving one another, even as God in Christ forgave you" (NKJV)*.

Here are seven practices that can help you live a life free from resentment and full of compassion, in harmony with God's teachings:

1. **Introspection** is an essential step in this process. Take time to reflect on moments from the past when you successfully forgave someone and recall the sense of relief that followed. Keep those memories close as a source of encouragement for the future. Introspection helps us reconnect with our inner self and reminds us that forgiveness is not only possible but healing.

2. To fully embrace forgiveness, it's important to anchor ourselves in God. **Daily prayer** is a powerful tool for experiencing His presence and guidance. Set aside moments to ask the Holy Spirit for help with the process of forgiveness. Meditate on Bible verses that talk about forgiveness, like *Ephesians 4:32,*

which encourages us to be kind, tender-hearted, and forgiving. Also, surround yourself with fellow believers. Joining a prayer group or participating in Bible studies where stories of forgiveness are shared can provide much-needed support and encouragement.

3. It's equally important to manage negative emotions and resist holding on to bitterness. Break the chains that bind you to resentment and offer full forgiveness. A simple yet effective practice for overcoming bitterness is **gratitude**. Write down a few things you're thankful for each day. This shift in focus can transform your perspective and it can help you appreciate the positive aspects of life. Gratitude opens the heart to joy and healing, as well as engaging in activities that bring you joy—whether it's spending time with loved ones or pursuing hobbies—thus keeping negativity at bay.

4. **Do not seek revenge.** When someone wrongs you, respond with kindness. The Bible encourages us to extend grace even to our enemies: *"If your enemy is hungry, give him bread to eat; And if he is thirsty, give him water to drink"* (Romans 12:20, NKJV). Jesus gave us the Golden Rule, found in Matthew 7:12 (NKJV): *"Therefore, whatever you want men to do to you, do also to them."* This should guide all of our relationships, offering us a way to respond with love and compassion, even in the face of hurt.

5. **Offer and accept compassion:** As we extend compassion to others, it's equally important to show it to ourselves. When you look at those who have hurt you through a lens of

kindness, you not only recognise their pain but also your own. Understanding others' actions requires empathy, but it must start with yourself. Ask yourself how you would feel in their place, but also how you react to your own mistakes and struggles. Just as you offer practical help to others—be it emotional or material—make sure you are providing the same care for yourself when needed.

6. **Forgiveness** opens the path to freedom from the burden of bitterness. To experience true forgiveness, it's essential to follow a process: first, acknowledge your own pain; then, seek to understand the other person's motives; next, express your feelings openly; and finally, let go of resentment. Letting go of grudges is like releasing a weight from your heart, and it creates space for healing and compassion to flourish.

7. In addition to emotional healing, forgiveness has profound benefits for your physical and mental wellbeing. **Letting go of resentment** can lower your stress levels and improve your overall sense of peace. Methods like writing a letter of forgiveness (even if you never send it) or participating in counselling can help you process and release the negative feelings you've been carrying. The act of releasing those emotions is not just freeing—it's transformative.

To live a life that reflects God's character, it is vital that we cultivate compassion in every area of our lives. This compassion not only draws us closer to others but also transforms us, helping us become more empathetic, kind-hearted, and aligned with our Creator. Here are some key areas where we can express divine compassion:

1. Compassion in suffering

When we suffer, true compassion requires that we respond to hurt not with revenge, but with kindness and understanding. This means we should not let our own wounds prevent us from seeing the humanity in others, and we should always seek to ease their suffering, even when we are hurting ourselves. For example, if someone has hurt you, instead of reacting with anger or planning revenge, try to understand what may have driven them to act that way. Perhaps they, too, are struggling. Respond with kindness, or, if necessary, distance yourself with grace, without worsening the conflict. Jesus gave us the perfect example of compassion when, even as He hung on the cross, He prayed for those who crucified Him: *"Father, forgive them, for they do not know what they do" (Luke 23:34, NKJV).*

2. Compassion in material matters

"But whoever has this world's goods, and sees his brother in need, and shuts up his heart from him, how does the love of God abide in him? My little children, let us not love in word or in tongue, but in deed and in truth" (1 John 3:17-18, NKJV).

Compassion is more than words; it calls for action. We need to offer tangible help to those in need, without expecting anything in return. This means opening our hearts not only to those close to us, but also to those who might be different from us or even those who have wronged us. In a divided world, material compassion could mean offering support to someone who may not share your views or beliefs, or simply lending a helping hand to a neighbour you may not always get along with, without judging them[83].

3. Compassion through sacrifice

True compassion involves being willing to put aside your own needs in order to help others. It means being able to see others not just as competitors, but as brothers and sisters in need of support. For example, when someone requires help and you have the means to offer it, take that step without hesitation even if it costs you time, energy, or resources. Every act of generosity becomes an opportunity to grow in the spirit of compassion. Jesus Himself demonstrated this ultimate compassion through the greatest sacrifice of all: giving His life so that we might be saved., When tied to sacrifice, compassion reflects the heart of the Gospel.

4. Compassion in spiritual matters

Compassion in the spiritual realm means supporting those who are struggling with their faith or going through inner battles, without judging or condemning them. Instead of rebuking those who doubt or face crises of faith, we are called to walk alongside them with empathy and understanding. For example, if someone is wrestling with doubt or questioning their beliefs, listen without judgement. Share your own experiences—how you have overcome similar moments of struggle—not to

---

[83] Peter Singer, *The Life You Can Save: How to Do Your Part to End World Poverty* (New York: Random House, 2009).

pressure them into your way of thinking but to offer hope and companionship. This kind of spiritual compassion can bring deep healing to those experiencing turmoil.

5. Compassion in your own experience

"Above all, love each other deeply, because love covers over a multitude of sins" (1 Peter 4:8, NKJV).

Compassion also means being open about your own mistakes and hardships, so that others can learn from them and avoid similar pitfalls. It's not about hiding or minimising problems but showing that we are all imperfect and can grow from our failures. For example, when someone is going through something you have personally experienced, share how you managed to overcome it. Do this with humility and sincerity, not from a place of superiority, but to encourage and inspire them to find hope and solutions.

6. Compassion in communication

In a world where gossip and slander are all too common, compassion in communication means being mindful of your words and refusing to contribute to the spread of negativity or false information. Choose to speak kindly and uplift those around you. For example, in your daily conversations, resist the temptation to engage in gossip. If someone is being spoken of negatively, try to find something positive to say about them or steer the conversation toward something constructive. Listening actively is also an essential part of compassionate communication. It allows you to truly understand the needs and feelings of others. Practise listening with your full attention, not just hearing the words but connecting with the emotions and experiences behind them.

7. Compassion in expectations

Compassion in our expectations means not expecting perfection from others and recognising that everyone has their own limitations. Adjust your expectations of people and accept their imperfections, just as you would hope to be accepted yourself. For example, in your relationships, remind yourself that we all make mistakes and that no one is perfect. If someone falls short of your expectations, rather than feeling disappointed or angry, try to approach the situation with understanding and empathy, remembering that you, too, have moments where you don't meet expectations.

By practising compassion in all these areas, we contribute to healing the social wounds that divide us and we create an environment where everyone feels respected and supported. These steps help us become empathetic and merciful people, embodying the character that God desires for us.

Walk humbly with Him, love mercy, and do justice. In this pursuit of divine justice and goodness, you will find true happiness.

Chapter 12

⌘

Those Who Will See God

"Blessed are the pure in heart, for they shall see God" (Matthew 5:8, NKJV).

One of the Bible verses that underlines the essence of the path to true happiness is found in the Book of Proverbs: *"Keep your heart with all diligence, for out of it spring the issues of life" (Proverbs 4:23, NKJV)*. In Hebrew, the term *libeha*, derived from the concept of lev, does not refer strictly to the physical heart, but to the mind, the core of human existence, encompassing thoughts, emotions, and intentions. In ancient times, the heart was considered the nucleus of life, because its rhythm seemed to reflect a person's emotional state and health. Therefore, the heart symbolises the emotional and intellectual centre of a person, and the biblical text speaks to the necessity of guarding our mind and soul.

As we enter the sixth antechamber of our spiritual journey, we will focus on a profound message etched on its front: *"Blessed are the pure in heart" (Matthew 5:8, NKJV)*. This statement raises two essential questions: How can we have a pure mind? And how can we see God?

Why is the mind so important in this process? Our mind is not only the place where thoughts take shape, but the centre where our values, beliefs, and attitudes are formed—those that guide us in every aspect of life. Beyond rational thought, the mind stores memories and emotions that influence how we see the world and how we react to it. For instance, someone raised in a critical environment may develop negative beliefs about themselves, which can affect their confidence and relationships. The mind defines our identity and directs how we interact with everything around us[84].

For this reason, it is essential to cleanse and transform our mind. Over time, we accumulate unhealthy or limiting thoughts and beliefs, either from difficult experiences or negative influences in our environment. Transforming the mind involves identifying these harmful patterns and replacing them with positive, constructive thoughts and attitudes. Through this process, we can change our perspective, improve our relationships, and live a happier, more balanced life.

---

[84] Daniel J. Siegel, *The Mindful Brain: Reflection and Attunement in the Cultivation of Well-Being* (New York: W.W. Norton & Company, 2007), pp. 28-32.

A pure mind allows us to see clearly what truly matters in life and brings us closer to God[85].

Throughout history, in many cultures and religious traditions, people have sought to understand and connect with a divine or transcendent force. Even in atheistic or neo-atheistic contexts, where the existence of a deity is rejected, people continue to search for the meaning of life and to explore what it means to be a higher being. In some interpretations of these perspectives, humanity is seen as having the potential to define its own destiny and rediscover itself, seeking to uncover what truly makes a being superior[86].

A biblical example that illustrates this concept is when Philip, one of the disciples, asks to see God the Father (John 14:8). Jesus replies: *"Have I been with you so long, and yet you have not known Me, Philip? He who has seen Me has seen the Father" (John 14:9, NKJV)*. This interaction highlights a common misunderstanding in comprehending the Trinity. In their attempt to grasp the divine mystery, some believe that Jesus Christ, God the Father, and the Holy Spirit are one and the same person, merely changing forms in front of humanity. This notion, known as **modalism**, denies the clear distinctions

---

[85] Carol S. Dweck, *Mindset: The New Psychology of Success* (New York: Random House, 2006), pp. 45-50.

[86] Charles Taylor, *A Secular Age* (Cambridge, MA: Belknap Press of Harvard University Press, 2007), pp. 25-30.

between the three Persons of the Trinity, each having a distinct role in the divine plan[87].

However, in the above passage, Jesus does not suggest a physical identity between Himself and the Father, but rather a perfect unity of will, purpose, and action. Jesus Christ faithfully reflects the character and will of the Father, not because He is a temporary manifestation of the Father, but because there is a profound and perfect communion between them. His actions, words, and thoughts are in complete alignment with what the Father has revealed to Him, and this harmony is an expression of the deep understanding and divine commitment that Jesus has taken upon Himself in representing the Father to the world.

We, too, can see God if we have a pure mind aligned with the divine will. This requires constant effort and involves letting go of the things that distort our perspective and prevent us from seeing God clearly.

When you began school and learned to write, you had to give up many things that brought you joy—your toys, time spent on the computer, or other fun activities. In their place, you invested time and effort into practising lines and strokes,

---

[87] Millard J. Erickson, *Christian Theology* (Grand Rapids, MI: Baker Academic, 2013), pp. 343-346.

which later became letters. This process wasn't easy, but it was necessary for developing your skills.

Similarly, to have a pure heart and to see the Lord Jesus, you must develop a different mindset, which is essential in the process of self-discovery. This transformation begins with the desire to see God reflected in yourself and to find true happiness. Only then can you take the next important step—learning how to change your mind. This process, known as **repentance** or the renewal of the mind, is something we explored in detail in Chapter 4.

The renewal of the mind and repentance are not simple emotional actions or verbal declarations made in the heat of the moment. It is a profound, ongoing process of inner transformation. Genuine repentance requires passing through the earlier stages, a spiritual journey through which you gradually let go of what keeps you away from God and cultivate an open and pure heart.

The Beatitudes described in the Gospel of Matthew are traits of an authentic believer, serving as a spiritual mirror in which we can examine ourselves. Like a recipe, they help us check whether we've followed the necessary steps. This reflection can be uncomfortable because it forces us to confront the areas where we've fallen short or allowed our ego to take control.

We live in an age where Christianity tends to be more philosophical than practical. We often say things we don't fully understand and claim concepts we don't truly live. We fail to realise that the Beatitudes follow a logical order, and we can't skip straight to the final stage without progressing through all the others. Each part of the journey has an entrance and an exit, and only the exit door leads to the next stage.

To reach a pure mind, we must engage in a continuous process of spiritual cleansing. Scripture reminds us that we were born in sin *(Psalm 51:5, NKJV)*, and without this cleansing, we will remain trapped in our sins. But cleansing the mind doesn't mean living a life without mistakes, as this is impossible. Even the most devoted believers are prone to falls, but this does not mean they cannot have a heart purified by God.

To ensure that we are actively involved in the process of changing and transforming our minds, here are a few key considerations:

1. The metamorphosis of the mind: a continuous process

The Bible tells us: *"Blessed are the pure in heart, for they shall see God" (Matthew 5:8, NKJV)*. This blessing is not just a distant promise but a direct call to action. It invites us to seek that inner purity, like gold hidden deep within the earth.

Even within us, burdened as we are by mistakes and imperfections, lie neglected spiritual treasures.

If we rediscover and cultivate them, they can lead us to a life of holiness and communion with God. The inner transformation begins with our minds.

Spiritual transformation is not merely about changing outward behaviours. It requires a profound reconfiguration of how we perceive life, our values, and how we relate to God and others. The Apostle Paul urges us not to conform to this age but to be transformed by the renewing of our minds so that we may discern *"the good and acceptable and perfect will of God" (Romans 12:2, NKJV)*. This transformation of the mind is essential for reflecting divine values in every aspect of our lives.

It's important to understand that this process of spiritual metamorphosis doesn't happen overnight.

This transformation is not a single event, but a long and continuous journey that requires effort, perseverance, and total dedication to the goal of living in accordance with God's will.

Each stage of this process is crucial and cannot be skipped. Just as the transformation of a caterpillar into a butterfly follows a sequential process, so must we pass through every necessary step to achieve holiness and inner purity. True transformation demands deep and unwavering commitment, even though absolute perfection is unattainable in this life.

Although perfection is beyond reach, that doesn't mean we should abandon our efforts. Just as the angels cover their faces in the presence of divine holiness, acknowledging that only God is perfect, we, too, must continually strive. The Apostle Paul encourages us to rise after each fall and keep running toward our spiritual goal: *"Not that I have already attained, or am already perfected; but I press on, that I may lay hold of that for which Christ Jesus has also laid hold of me" (Philippians 3:12, NKJV).* Faith is not a leisurely walk but an intense race, fully aware of the promised reward at the end—the gift of divine grace.

A true believer is not defined by having reached perfection, but by the fact that God continuously supports them in their spiritual journey. God always upholds those who, with faith and perseverance, continue to move forward, even if they have not yet attained perfection.

This spiritual journey is filled with challenges, but also brings deep joy and spiritual satisfaction. With every step forward, we move closer to our divine goal—living a life of holiness and complete dedication to God. Though the road is long and difficult, it leads to an authentic communion with our Creator and a life rich in meaning.

2. A living sacrifice: a life of holiness

The Apostle Paul exhorts us to offer our bodies as a *"living sacrifice, holy and acceptable to God" (Romans 12:1, NKJV).* This command goes beyond merely giving up certain pleasures or habits—it represents a deep, active commitment to living a life that honours God in every aspect. A "living sacrifice" means action: a life of faith expressed through deeds and behaviours that reflect God's will.

Holiness is not just about the absence of sin, but about total dedication to divine purposes. To be holy means to be set apart for God, living not for personal pleasure, but to honour Him in everything we do. This requires an active commitment to our faith, living each day in accordance with divine principles.

A living sacrifice is a life lived in obedience and dedication to God. Every thought, every word, and every action should be directed toward glorifying Him.

This is the profound meaning of the Christian life: a life of holiness and devotion, where we are always ready to sacrifice our own desires to fulfil God's will.

3. Active listening: the key to transformation

To truly transform, we must be receptive to God's guidance and apply it in our lives. Active listening doesn't just involve hearing God's words, but acting on them. It is a listening that manifests in deeds and real change in our lives. As the Apostle James reminds us: *"But be doers of the word, and not hearers only, deceiving yourselves" (James 1:22, NKJV).*

We often receive valuable advice and divine guidance, but we leave it unapplied. It's like a precious book which, left unopened on a shelf, loses its practical value. Similarly, divine instructions lose their significance if we don't integrate them into our lives. Active listening is the key to a new life, transforming theoretical knowledge of divine teachings into practical application.

Listening is not a passive act, but an active commitment to align our lives with God's will. It requires deliberate focus and a constant effort to pause from the daily hustle and truly listen to His voice. Through active listening, we manage to tune in to the "frequency" of the divine, gaining clarity and spiritual direction.

4. Obstacles to transformation

One of the greatest obstacles to transformation is our attachment to old habits and mindsets. Change is often seen as uncomfortable and difficult, which makes us resist it. It's easier to cling to what we know, even if it isn't beneficial, than to open ourselves to the unknown and risk changing.

There is also a tendency to underestimate our ability to transform. We believe that certain changes are impossible or that we are not strong enough to make them. But Scripture teaches us that through God's strength, all things are possible *(Philippians 4:13, NKJV)*. Obstacles that seem insurmountable can be overcome through faith, prayer, and obedience to God's will.

To truly transform, we must be willing to detach ourselves from the comfort of the familiar and open ourselves to change. This involves a constant adjustment of the mind and heart to align with God's will, allowing Him to shape and transform us.

5. Applied wisdom: living a life of faith

Every decision and action should be guided by God's wisdom, not only to ensure that we live according to His will, but also to enhance our everyday life and relationships with others. Applying divine teachings is not an occasional exercise, but a continuous discipline that helps us stay on the right path.

In this quest for divine wisdom, it is essential to distance ourselves from the distractions and temptations of modern life. The daily noise and constant influx of information can prevent us from hearing God's voice. This is why we must take time to meditate on divine teachings and apply them to our lives. True wisdom comes from a deep, active relationship with God, and this manifests through a life lived in obedience and integrity.

The Apostle Paul urges us not to conform to this world, but to be transformed by the renewal of our minds, so that we may discern *"the good, acceptable, and perfect will of God" (Romans 12:2, NKJV)*. This transformation is not a quick or easy process; it requires time, effort, dedication, and a deep desire to align ourselves with the divine will.

In a world that constantly pressures us to conform to its norms, the transformation of the mind becomes a sacred act of rebellion, a rejection of superficiality and a call to authenticity.

To live an authentic life of faith, it's important to be attentive to what God is telling us and to respond through action. This active listening and application of divine teachings help us grow spiritually and move closer to our divine purpose. In doing so, our lives become a living testimony to God's grace and power, and our inner transformation reflects His ongoing work within us.

6. A pure mind (heart) through transformation

A pure heart is not only a symbol of innocence, but also represents a life completely dedicated to God—a heart cleansed by His forgiveness and lived in obedience to His will. This involves a continuous transformation, a process in which we abandon our old ways and open ourselves to a new life, centred on holiness and devotion to God.

Spiritual transformation is a challenging path, but it is the only way to live an authentic and meaningful life, where we can fully experience God's presence and blessing. With each step forward, we draw closer to our divine purpose and to eternal communion with our Creator.

Chapter 13

The Mind that is
More Valuable than Gold

"Keep your heart with all diligence,
for out of it spring the issues of life"
(Proverbs 4:23, NKJV).

In this chapter, we will explore how to develop a wise mind and adopt the right attitude so that our lives truly reflect the authenticity of our faith. As we seek genuine happiness, it is essential to align our lives with the clear principles the Saviour has revealed to us. To achieve this, we must unlearn the old mindset that led us to failure and relearn a new one – the divine mindset. Romans 12:2 (NKJV) urges us not to conform to societal trends and norms that we often adopt without critical thought, but to be transformed by the renewing of our minds.

Authentic faith is not blind and does not emerge out of nowhere. It is the result of a conscious process of understanding and practical application. A powerful example of this is David's prayer: *"Create in me a clean heart, O God, and renew a steadfast spirit within me. Do not cast me away from Your presence, and do not take Your Holy Spirit from me. Restore to me the joy of Your salvation, and uphold me by Your generous Spirit"* (Psalm 51:10-12, NKJV). This prayer reveals David's deep desire for a transformed mind, aligned with the divine will. In Hebrew culture, the term *lev* does not refer only to the heart as a physical organ, but also to the mind – the centre of human thought and emotion. David asks God not only for inner cleansing but also for mental and spiritual stability, which is essential for living according to God's purpose. This prayer emphasises that true joy and stability come from salvation and the work that only the Creator can do within us.

Therefore, the call to maintain a pure mind is not merely a moral decision, but a vital spiritual requirement.

A pure mind is the foundation of an authentic relationship with God and with others. It is the source from which divine wisdom, spiritual discernment, and the ability to live according to God's will flow. Without this inner transformation, all our actions remain superficial, lacking depth and a real connection to the source of life – God.

To prepare the mind to reflect divine wisdom in all aspects of our lives, we must understand that true wisdom comes from correct knowledge. Psalm 119 (NKJV) offers us a clear perspective: *"Your testimonies are wonderful; therefore, my soul keeps them. The entrance of Your words gives light; it gives understanding to the simple" (Psalm 119:129-130, NKJV).* These verses highlight that not only that which we learn is important, but also the source from which we draw our knowledge. The source of our knowledge is vital because from it comes the wisdom and light needed to navigate life's challenges. The wisdom we seek must be anchored in truth and lead us toward a life lived in accordance with God's will.

Another essential aspect is the ancient command deeply rooted in Jewish culture: *"Keep your heart with all diligence, for out of it spring the issues of life" (Proverbs 4:23, NKJV).* This command reminds us of the need to guard our mind, as it influences all the actions and decisions we make. In the previous chapter, we discussed Paul's exhortation to be transformed by the renewing of our minds (Romans 12:2, NKJV). This transformation is crucial because our thinking plays a fundamental role in our spiritual success. To develop a mind filled with divine wisdom, we must build on a solid foundation that provides all the resources we need to live according to divine teaching.

The transformation of the mind is not limited to accumulating knowledge; it must also include applying that knowledge in our daily lives.

———————• •———————

A wise mind can only be cultivated
by putting the teachings of Jesus Christ
into practice.

———————• •———————

It is important not to be mere passive listeners or admirers of His words but to live them actively, applying them in all aspects of our lives. This active commitment to divine teaching transforms us from within and helps us reflect God's wisdom in everything we do.

To develop a wise mind, here are some essential principles to remember:

1. Let go of pride and prejudice! (Matthew 5:3, NKJV)

Pride often stands in the way of gaining wisdom. We are tempted to think we are too good to learn from others whom we perceive as inferior. To become wise, we must open our hearts and acknowledge that we are all equal before God, and parts of the same body.

2. Be honest!

Denying reality does not solve problems. To overcome difficulties, we must face them with honesty and make decisions that lead to healing and spiritual growth.

3. Be teachable!

True wisdom comes from recognising our limits and being willing to learn every day, even from the most unexpected sources. Be open to learning in any context, acknowledging that every experience can bring a valuable lesson.

4. Hunger and thirst for truth!

The thirst for knowledge must be directed toward the authentic source that leads to righteousness. We must cultivate a deep desire to seek truth and righteousness so that our inner transformation is complete and genuine.

By adopting an attitude of total dedication to God, we will discover that we are better protected from the traps of the modern world. In a world where many rush recklessly into uncertain directions, believers equipped with divine wisdom will have the ability to carefully evaluate each step. This vigilance will not only protect us from mistakes, but will also provide us with a distinct clarity of mind and a clear vision of our purpose in life.

Wise people generally appear healthier and more vigorous than those who neglect the spiritual and intellectual aspects of their existence.

This health is not accidental; it is the result of a balanced lifestyle, where excesses are avoided, and the desire for spiritual and intellectual growth prevails over purely physical temptations. A healthy body often reflects a healthy and disciplined mind, one dedicated to a life lived in harmony with the Creator's will[88].

God desires that we seek wisdom and actively engage in this pursuit. According to the Oxford English Dictionary, being proactive means taking action to make a difference in the world. This divine call urges us to be active agents of change, positively influencing society through our actions and thoughts. If we draw near to God, He will draw near to us (James 4:8, NKJV). A purified heart and mind become the foundation upon which we can build a life of commitment, without hesitation or doubt, and guided by a clear and undivided vision.

The Saviour left us a profound parable about the importance of a clear and undivided perspective: *"The lamp of the body is the eye. If therefore your eye is good, your whole body will be full of light. But if your eye is bad, your whole body will be full of darkness"* (Matthew 6:22-23, NKJV).

Why does Jesus use the concept of a singular eye? Typically, both eyes look in the same direction and function together, forming a unified image. In a healthy body, the eyes coordinate perfectly, focusing on the same objective. This metaphor shows us how important a clear and undivided perspective is in

---

[88] Koenig, Harold G. "Religion, Spirituality, and Health: The Research and Clinical Implications." *ISRN Psychiatry* vol. 2012 (2012): 278730. doi:10.5402/2012/278730.

our spiritual lives. Just as healthy eyes focus on the same im-age, our minds must be oriented toward a single goal – living according to divine values, ethics, and morals.

This leads us to the idea of an undivided mind, which is purified and ready to stay away from sin. God calls us to be proactive in maintaining this mental purity. This requires continuous focus on the mindset of Christ, regardless of the temptations surrounding us. The process of sanctification is an ongoing one, unfolding throughout our entire lives. In this spiritual journey, we constantly refine our vision and attitude toward life and the world, gradually transforming into the im-age that God desires for us.

Sanctification involves a deep and ongoing relationship with God, in which our minds become increasingly aligned with His will.

The consequences of this dedication are evident: when we listen to God's call and no longer have a divided heart, but are ready to fully commit to Him, divine wisdom will be found in us through the knowledge and mindset we have gained from God's Word. This is the transformation that turns a narrow, imitative faith into one that is authentic and profound, guided by a mind that has understood spiritual reality. As the main coordinator of the body, the mind must lead, not be led by bodily desires.

Do you want your mind to be wise and more valuable than gold? This is built by absorbing divine values, responding to the call to prepare your body and mind to access the knowledge of truth and adopt the divine mindset, then applying it in everyday life.

You will need a wise faith – one that is connected to your thinking, and your thinking should be connected to the understanding of God and His good, acceptable, and perfect will (Romans 12:2, NKJV). The secret of a wise mind lies in the deep understanding of God's will.

As it is defined by the Oxford English Dictionary, the mind is the superior faculty of the brain that reflects the surrounding reality through concepts, judgments, and theories. While it is the driving force of our thoughts, this does not automatically guarantee wisdom. There is a fundamental difference between intelligence and wisdom. Intelligence refers to the ability to understand things, solve problems, and analyse situations based on knowledge and experience. Wisdom, on the other hand, involves applying this knowledge in an ethical and responsible way, taking moral values into account[89].

For example, a person may possess remarkable intelligence, but without solid ethical principles, that intelligence can

---

[89] Sternberg, Robert J. *Wisdom, Intelligence, and Creativity Synthesized.* Cambridge University Press, 2003.

be used in destructive ways. History shows that in the 1940s and 1950s, highly intelligent scientists contributed to the development of nuclear weapons. Although these discoveries represented significant advances in science and technology, their use had devastating consequences, illustrating how the lack of a moral compass can turn intelligence into a destructive force.

Thus, born from a deep understanding of ethical and moral values, wisdom is essential to ensure that our intelligence is used for the common good, not for destruction. Thought must be guided by wisdom, and wisdom is learned from the Word of God: *"Hear, my son, and receive my sayings, and the years of your life will be many. I have taught you in the way of wisdom; I have led you in right paths. When you walk, your steps will not be hindered, and when you run, you will not stumble. Take firm hold of instruction, do not let go; keep her, for she is your life"* (Proverbs 4:10-13, NKJV).

Prepare your mindset, character, and body so that they accumulate the knowledge of God. In this process, it is essential to be aware of the cultural context we live in, as modern Christianity has been influenced by two fundamental errors.

The first error is the over-spiritualisation of wisdom. Hosea 4:6 (NKJV) tells us: *"My people are destroyed for lack of knowledge."* It is crucial not to interpret everything solely through a spiritual lens without also analysing and understanding rationally what is happening around us. God calls us to understand why certain events occur and what He wants to communicate through them. In this way, our wisdom will grow, and we will become better equipped to face life's challenges without being swept away by external influences.

The second error is the **devaluation of wisdom**. 1 Peter 1:13 (NKJV) tells us: *"Therefore gird up the loins of your mind, be sober, and rest your hope fully upon the grace that is to be brought to you at the revelation of Jesus Christ."* In a world saturated with information and various influences, it is essential to discern between worldly wisdom and divine wisdom. The wisdom that comes from God offers us a deeper and clearer perspective on life. Some suggest that we should believe without asking questions or seeking deeper answers. This approach can lead to a distorted understanding of faith, as true faith does not exclude critical thinking and the pursuit of wisdom. On the contrary, God encourages us to grow our faith through knowledge and wisdom.

When Christ says, *"I am the Alpha and the Omega"* (Revelation 1:8, NKJV), He emphasises that He is the beginning and the end of all things, including knowledge. Through studying and reflecting on the Word, we enrich our minds and hearts, cultivating a faith that not only accepts but also understands deeply. Therefore, we should not be content with phrases like *"The Lord knows best,"* without seeking deeper understanding, but should dedicate ourselves to learning and deepening divine knowledge. Wisdom is not something to fear or avoid, but a divine gift that helps us understand God's will.

Rather than relying on simplistic interpretations or external influences, we will learn to follow the subtle guidance that comes from a deep and personal relationship with God.

Here are seven essential principles that, once applied to your life, will cultivate an authentic mind and a wisdom more valuable than gold:

Principle 1 – Distinguish between trusting someone and truly relying on them

"Let not your heart be troubled; you believe in God, believe also in Me" (John 14:1, NKJV).

In a world filled with numerous opinions and information, one of the greatest challenges is understanding the difference between trusting what someone says and truly relying on that person. Often, we limit ourselves to listening to advice or ideas from those around us – friends, family, or community leaders. However, to live an authentic and meaningful life, it is essential to not only pay attention to what others say, but to also develop our own convictions, based on direct and real experiences[90].

True trust does not mean mere passive acceptance of what others tell us. It manifests in an authentic relationship, where we are actively involved and can truly rely on someone for support, guidance, and understanding. This distinction between superficial trust and deep trust is vital for our personal growth. True trust requires a solid relationship and direct knowledge, not just information passed down from others. This provides

---

[90] Robert B. Cialdini, *Influence: The Psychology of Persuasion* (New York: Harper Business, 2006).

us with the stability needed to navigate life's challenges, knowing we rely on something real and dependable.

Similarly, in our spiritual lives, it is not enough to rely solely on what others have told us about faith or spirituality. It is essential to experience it personally and build a direct relationship with the source of our faith. Thus, we move from theoretical knowledge to practical and authentic living, which transforms and shapes our lives. This is not a formal relationship, but a deep and intimate one that gives us the strength to lean on God in the difficult moments of life.

Principle 2 – Acknowledge your mistakes and be honest with yourself

One of the essential aspects of personal and spiritual growth is the ability to acknowledge mistakes and be honest with ourselves. In a society that emphasises success and outward image, it can be difficult to accept that we have made mistakes or have weaknesses. However, true growth begins when we are willing to look honestly within ourselves and recognise where we have failed.

Confessing mistakes is not only an act of humility, but also a crucial step toward liberation and healing. When we are honest with ourselves, we free ourselves from the burden of lies and self-deception, opening our hearts to change. This honesty allows us to identify areas in our lives that need improvement and to actively work on becoming better people[91].

Confession also plays an important role in our relationships with others. When we open up and acknowledge our mistakes, we inspire others to do the same. This creates an environment of trust and mutual support, where we can all learn from our mistakes and grow together. Confession can also be the first step toward reconciliation and healing in damaged relationships, allowing us to build stronger and healthier connections.

Spiritually, confession is a fundamental practice that helps keep our hearts pure and open to transformation. By sincerely confessing our mistakes, we reconnect to our source of inner strength and open the way to a more authentic and fulfilled life.

Principle 3 – Let your life be guided by solid principles, not external influences

"Through Your precepts I get understanding... Your word is a lamp to my feet and a light to my path" (Psalm 119:104-105, NKJV).

In a world filled with information and influences from all directions, it is easy to be swayed by what others tell us. However, to live an authentic and meaningful life, it is essential to

---

[91] Brown, Brené. *The Gifts of Imperfection: Let Go of Who You Think You're Supposed to Be and Embrace Who You Are.* Hazelden Publishing, 2010.

guide ourselves by solid principles and core values, not just by external influences or fleeting trends.

Living according to solid principles means basing our decisions and actions on deeply rooted beliefs that reflect who we truly are and what we aim to achieve in life. This requires deep reflection, self-analysis, and a commitment to living in alignment with our values, even when it is difficult or unpopular.

Rather than being carried by the current of public opinion or social pressures, we must build a value system that guides us through life's challenges and opportunities. This value system provides the stability we need to remain true to our convictions, even in the face of adversity. It helps us maintain our integrity and make decisions that are in alignment with who we are and what we believe in.

Spiritually speaking, guiding our lives by solid principles means being led by divine wisdom, which comes from reflecting on the Word and personal study. It is important not to be swayed by the opinions of others without critically analysing them and comparing them with our own values and convictions. This allows us to live an authentic and meaningful life, where our actions are aligned with who we are and what we truly believe.

Principle 4 – Commit to continuously improving your spiritual life

"Let a man so consider us, as servants of Christ and stewards of the mysteries of God" (1 Corinthians 4:1, NKJV).

Personal and spiritual development is a continuous process that requires dedication and constant effort. No one reaches a state of spiritual or personal perfection overnight; it is a long journey filled with lessons and challenges. A clear understanding of who we are and our place in the world helps us consciously engage in this process of constant growth.

The commitment to continuously improving our spiritual life involves dedicating time for reflection, prayer, and meditation on the Word, always seeking to learn and grow. This may include reading studies, attending seminars or personal and spiritual development courses, or engaging in activities that help us connect more deeply with ourselves and with God.

It is important to recognise that this growth process is not linear. There will be moments of stagnation, regression, or doubt. However, it is precisely in these moments that our commitment to growth is tested and strengthened. Perseverance in the face of challenges and constant dedication to improving our spiritual lives are essential for living a meaningful and fulfilled life.

Moreover, the commitment to improving our spiritual life positively impacts those around us. When we strive to live an authentic and integrity-filled life, we positively influence those in our church and contribute to creating a healthier and stronger environment. Through our example, we can inspire others to follow their own path of growth and seek to live more authentic and fulfilled lives.

Principle 5 – Sincerely ask for help in difficult moments

"Create in me a clean heart, O God, and renew a steadfast spirit within me. Do not cast me away from Your presence, and do not take Your Holy Spirit from me. Restore to me the joy of Your salvation, and uphold me by Your generous Spirit" *(Psalm 51:10-12, NKJV).*

In difficult moments, we are often tempted to face challenges alone without asking for help. However, the ability to ask for help when needed is not a sign of weakness, but of maturity and wisdom. No one can succeed alone in every aspect of life, and recognising this is essential for our personal and spiritual growth.

Prayer and meditation on the Word can be powerful tools that connect us to our inner source of strength. When we pray sincerely, we acknowledge our need for help and open ourselves to divine support.

This act of humility keeps our hearts open and reconnects us to what is truly important.

We must also be willing to ask for help not only from God, but also from those around us. Friends, family, mentors, or counsellors can play an essential role in supporting us in difficult times. Asking for help is an act of courage and wisdom that opens up new perspectives and solutions, helping us overcome obstacles and continue our journey with more strength and clarity.

Principle 6 – Stay consistent with your ethical and moral beliefs

"Therefore I will look to the Lord; I will wait for the God of my salvation; my God will hear me" (Micah 7:7, NKJV).

One of the greatest challenges in modern life is remaining consistent in our beliefs and values, despite external pressures and influences. In a society where trends change rapidly and where we are tempted to adopt what is popular or widely accepted, it can be difficult to remain true to our convictions.

Perseverance in our divine beliefs and values is essential for living an authentic and meaningful life. This means not allowing ourselves to be swayed by what is fashionable or by the opinions of others, but maintaining our commitment to our fundamental values, even when it is difficult. Perseverance requires courage and dedication, but it provides us with the stability necessary to navigate life's challenges with integrity.

From a spiritual perspective, perseverance in beliefs and values means maintaining our commitment to what is truly important, regardless of circumstances. This includes staying committed to our faith, continuing our spiritual development, and living in accordance with biblical values, even in the face of adversity.

Principle 7 – Look to the future with optimism and confidence

"Behold what manner of love the Father has bestowed on us, that we should be called children of God! Therefore the world does not know us, because it did not know Him. Beloved, now we are children of God; and it has not yet been revealed what we shall be, but we know that when He is revealed, we shall be like Him, for we shall see Him as He is" (1 John 3:1-2, NKJV).

In a world full of uncertainties and challenges, it is easy to become overwhelmed by fear and doubt. However, having a positive and confident attitude towards the future helps us maintain hope and prepares us for what is to come.

———•—•———

Optimism does not mean ignoring difficulties or deceiving ourselves with illusions, but recognising that, regardless of the circumstances, we have the power to face challenges and build a better future.

———•—•———

This means focusing on opportunities, not obstacles, and trusting that our efforts will bring positive results. From a spiritual perspective, optimism is supported by the belief that there is a greater plan for our lives and that we are supported by God on this journey. This gives us the stability and courage to move forward, no matter the difficulties we encounter.

We conclude this chapter with an invitation filled with hope: if you want to develop a wise mind, capable of guiding you in this world as a true follower of Christ, make sure you are on the right foundation – the one God desires you to build this valuable mindset upon. With all the resources at your disposal, do not hesitate to transform your mind, accepting God's Word within you and allowing it to shape you.

Keep your eyes fixed on the goal, knowing that at the end of this journey, the prize of heavenly calling awaits you. God will give you this reward.

Chapter 14

⸎

Peacemakers

"Blessed are the peacemakers,
for they shall be called sons of God"
Matthew 5:9 (NKJV).

We have now arrived at the last of the **seven antechambers** of our inner journey, in our search for the mindset that can restore our lost happiness. Looking into the mirror of God's Word, we begin to distinguish this mindset and, with it, our true essence – the one that reflects the divine image. We also understand how a pure character and a correct attitude should look in a society that seems to have lost its direction. However, to reach this point, it was necessary to travel the arduous road of giving up old habits and thoughts that had become deeply rooted in our minds, rediscovering the beauty that the Creator has placed within us.

In this chapter, we will explore what it truly means to bring peace around us and why this attitude is essential for finding inner peace. At the forefront of this stage stands the inscription: *"Blessed are the peacemakers, for they shall be called sons of God" (Matthew 5:9, NKJV).*

To begin with, we must understand that peace does not merely mean the absence of conflict. It is a profound concept that includes harmony, wellbeing, and reconciliation – both with ourselves and with those around us.

*** *

Therefore, the ability to bring peace becomes a sign of spiritual maturity and a life lived in harmony with the divine will.

*** *

History teaches us that in the last 3,500 years, humanity has experienced only about 300 years of peace[92]. This statistic shows how rare humanity has enjoyed times of tranquillity, and even those were often marked by a fragile calm, far from true harmony. Peace is not merely the cessation of war; it is a state of balance in interpersonal and collective relationships.

In 1945, after two devastating world wars, humanity realised the danger of self-destruction and created the United

---

[92] Joshua S. Goldstein, *Winning the War on War: The Decline of Armed Conflict Worldwide* (New York: Dutton, 2011).

Nations (UN) to prevent conflicts and maintain global peace[93]. However, since the establishment of the UN, armed conflicts have continued to erupt in various parts of the world, revealing that maintaining peace is a constant challenge. Our generation faces the spectre of a Third World War, fuelled by a nuclear arsenal capable of destroying life on Earth many times over[94].

This reality raises a profound question: how have we come to carry within us the seeds of destruction rather than those of life? It challenges us to reflect on our choices, on how we manage power, and on the direction we have taken. It is a call to awareness and a fundamental change in how we relate to peace, to life, and to our responsibility for humanity's future. Only by cultivating inner peace and committing to being peace-makers can we hope to reverse this destructive trend and build a better future for all. *"Where do wars and fights come from among you? Do they not come from your desires for pleasure that war in your members?" (James 4:1, NKJV).*

This observation extends our analysis to a simple question: Why can we no longer be happy people in this world? The instinctive answer is to blame the society in which we live, forgetting that we are the ones who created it. We are the ones stumbling over our greed to become someone and our desire to climb as high as possible[95].

---

[93] Jussi M. Hanhimäki, *The United Nations: A Very Short Introduction*, Oxford University Press, 2015.

[94] Yuval Noah Harari, *21 Lessons for the 21st Century* (New York: Spiegel & Grau, 2018), pp. 82-85.

[95] Jonathan Haidt, *The Happiness Hypothesis: Finding Modern Truth in Ancient Wisdom*, Basic Books, 2006, p. 89.

Yet the secret to happiness has always been within our reach. An ancient text, wisdom thousands of years old, reminds us to *"Pursue peace with all people, and holiness, without which no one will see the Lord" (Hebrews 12:14, NKJV).* These two attributes – peace and holiness – are essential to our calling to live in peace, as 1 Corinthians 7:15 (NKJV) urges: "God has called us to peace".

Next, we will explore how all the knowledge and teachings accumulated must materialise in the concept of peace and the assumption of the role of peacemakers, true emissaries of the divine character.

To be a peacemaker does not only mean to spread peace, but to live it deeply.
You cannot offer what you do not have or speak about something you have not fully understood.

This final stage of our inner journey is also the most complex and difficult. You may often feel that although you strive to find the path of reconciliation, it is easier to choose the path of conflict. It is understandable. The mindset of a peacemaker represents the highest step in the evolution of the human mind and in the development of spirituality.

To truly become a peacemaker and – implicitly – a bringer of happiness, it is necessary to pass through all the previous stages of the spiritual journey.

Peace-making is the result of a mindset shaped by God over time.

This requires wisdom – not mere intelligence, but that profound wisdom that comes from above, as James 3:17 reminds us: *"But the wisdom that is from above is first pure, then peaceable, gentle, willing to yield, full of mercy and good fruits, without partiality and without hypocrisy" (NKJV)*. This wisdom is shaped gradually, as we allow ourselves to be guided by God.

As we advance in this learning process, the challenges will become more intense. Nevertheless, along the way, we will form a strong motivation: the closer we come to understanding and applying these teachings, the more we will resemble God. God has given us the peace that surpasses all worldly understanding, a deep inner calm: *"Peace I leave with you, My peace I give to you; not as the world gives do I give to you. Let not your heart be troubled..." (John 14:27, NKJV)*.

To fully understand what it means to be a promoter of peace, it is essential to clarify some fundamental concepts:

- What is the true meaning of peace, and how does it differ from a mere truce?

- Who is the person who promotes peace and is considered to live in the Spirit of God?

- What motivates people to become promoters of peace?

- What efforts are required to become a true person of peace?

- What are the outcomes that a promoter of peace should aim for?

By exploring these aspects, we will better understand our calling to become promoters of peace, and we will be better prepared to live in accordance with the divine values we cherish.

Imagine standing before the Creator, who asks you a single question: "What can I do for you?" How would you answer? Perhaps your mind will be overwhelmed with various options, such as security, peace, or justice. However, the essence of the Saviour's message to humanity is expressed in three simple exhortations: "Do not be afraid!", "Change your ways!", "Peace be with you!"

The shortest but most powerful sermon of Christ was: *"Repent, for the kingdom of heaven is at hand!" (Matthew 4:17, NKJV)*. This call to transformation changed the lives of many, inviting them to rethink their existence and find true inner peace. To live without fear, we must understand that God asks us to change our mindset. Once we transform our way of thinking, we will discover true peace.

Peace can seem like an unattainable ideal in the modern world. Anxiety and stress make it difficult to find inner balance, and tranquillity seems increasingly hard to achieve, both in our personal lives and in interpersonal relationships. Disputes arise at every step, and our society is often marked by tension. Looking around, we see a world in a constant state of turmoil.

However, Christ encouraged us with these words: *"These things I have spoken to you, that in Me you may have peace. In the world you will have tribulation; but be of good cheer, I have overcome the world"* *(John 16:33, NKJV)*. The peace offered by God is not just a temporary cessation of conflicts but a profound state of inner harmony, a calm that surpasses all worldly understanding.

The dictionary defines peace as a state of mutual understanding between nations, an agreement to cease hostilities. However, this represents only an external peace, a kind of truce that maintains appearances, but does not truly change people's hearts. In our society, peace is often seen as a pause in fighting, not as a genuine reconciliation.

Today, the global nuclear arsenal is powerful enough to destroy the Earth many times over. These weapons are kept as a threat – "If you attack me, I will respond with force." This is the world's view of peace: a fragile balance based on fear and threat, not on true understanding and reconciliation.

However, true peace, as God intended it, is not merely the absence of conflict. Divine peace means a state of wellbeing, fulfilment, and completeness.

To attain this peace, we must live our lives according to divine values. In the Old Testament, the concept of "shalom" is often mentioned, signifying not only the absence of war but complete restoration, the recovery of what has been lost. It is a peace that restores wholeness and brings back what was broken.

You may wonder if it is possible to "reset" yourself and become a new person. Yes, this is the profound meaning of "shalom" – complete restoration.

God promises us that, by drawing closer to Him, we can regain lost balance and renew our lives. Jesus calls us to experience this peace and to share it with others.

In the New Testament, the term "eirene" is used to denote peace, representing the outcome of restoration, that state of tranquillity that follows the process of repair. True peace does not come without this process of restoration. Peacemakers are those who, like Jesus, work to restore what has been broken.

We cannot become peacemakers without giving up pride and going through the necessary stages of spiritual growth. A proud person will not seek true peace, but only their own justification. To become peacemakers, we must change our way of thinking and prepare our souls to reflect divine peace.

Likewise, we cannot promote true peace if we focus only on our own sufferings and do not see the needs of those around us. Being a promoter of peace means giving up selfishness, controlling our impulses, and opening our hearts to understand and love others.

To become promoters of peace, we must truly desire to be like God, hungry and thirsty for His righteousness. Only then will we be able to experience true peace, not just a temporary truce.

True peace comes from our relationship with God, through faith. *"Therefore, having been justified by faith, we have peace with God through our Lord Jesus Christ" (Romans 5:1, NKJV)*. Peacemakers are those who have found this peace through Christ and are willing to share it with others. *"[...] and forgive us our debts, as we forgive our debtors" (Matthew 6:12, NKJV)*. Forgiveness is the key to experiencing true peace. Only when we forgive from the heart can we live in harmony with God and others, becoming true promoters of peace.

Here is how we can attain peace so that we may then become peacemakers:

1. **Reconciliation with God:** An essential step in the spiritual life is to be reconciled with God. You may feel that you have already done this when you asked Christ to forgive you, but it is important to reflect: what has happened since then? If you have sinned again, you should not be discouraged. Reconciliation with God is a continuous process, in which, every time we err, we return to Him for forgiveness. The Bible teaches us that those who are led by the Spirit of God are considered His children (Romans 8:14-15, NKJV). This means we are called to live in a constant relationship with God, always seeking to reconcile with Him and remain on His path.

2. **The continuous choice of peace:** Peace with God is not a singular event but a choice we make every day. It is important to distinguish between being reconciled with God and living daily in His peace. When Jesus died on the cross, He offered us reconciliation with God – a gift received through faith. However, to experience this peace daily, we must remain connected to its source, cultivating a constant relationship with God. As Scripture tells us: *"And the peace of God, which surpasses all understanding, will guard your hearts and minds through Christ Jesus"* (Philippians 4:6-7, NKJV). This peace comes when we choose to live in faith and prayer.

3. **Building a personal relationship with Christ:**
The relationship with Christ should not be formal or
distant but deep and personal, like a family relationship. We are not only servants of Christ; we are children of God, with all the dignity and rights that come
with this status. This means we are heirs of His Kingdom, and He considers us part of His family. Jesus said
to us: *"These things I have spoken to you, that in Me
you may have peace" (John 16:33, NKJV).* Authentic
peace comes from a deep, trusting relationship with
Christ, not just from intellectual knowledge of Him.
Once we become children of God, we will become more
and more like Him, reflecting His character and values
in our live.

4. **Constant communication with God:** Open communication with God is essential to maintain a living
and authentic relationship with Him. Do not hesitate
to talk to God about your desires and concerns, to tell
Him that you want to have peace with Him and in Him.
Prayer is a powerful means by which we connect to our
source of peace and inner strength. This constant communication helps us live a life anchored in faith and to
experience authentic peace.

5. **Releasing burdens through forgiveness:** To experience peace, it is essential to let go of the burdens
we carry – resentments, the desire for revenge, painful memories. Forgiveness is the key to releasing these

burdens and finding inner tranquillity. When we forgive, we not only free ourselves, but also release those who have wronged us. In this way, the chains that bind us to pain and bitterness are broken, allowing us to live in authentic peace.

6. **Entrusting worries into the Lord's hands**: Instead of focusing on the things we cannot change, it is wiser to focus on what we can control and leave the rest in God's hands. Scripture assures us that *"If God is for us, who can be against us?" (Romans 8:31, NKJV)*. This promise should bring us calm and assurance, knowing that God cares for us and provides His protection in all circumstances.

7. **Maintaining peace in times of trial:** Î7. In times of trial, peace can seem hard to achieve. However, the Lord Jesus invites us to come to Him for rest and to take His yoke, which is easy (Matthew 11:28-30, NKJV). This invitation assures us that, regardless of the difficulties we face, Christ is with us, offering the support and tranquillity we need. He promises to bear our burdens, but this does not mean we should be passive. We are called to bear one another's burdens, as Scripture teaches: *"Bear one another's burdens, and so fulfill the law of Christ" (Galatians 6:2, NKJV)*. In this way, we contribute to the peace and wellbeing of the community to which we belong.

8. Commitment to promoting peace: Being a promoter of peace means not only living in peace but also working actively to create and maintain peace around us. The Lord Jesus showed us how to do this by His example, bearing others' burdens and bringing peace into their lives. If we want to experience true happiness, we must go through the stages of spiritual growth and become practitioners of peace, even in the face of challenges. You may ask why you should bear others' burdens when you have just been freed from your own. Remember that when we reached the seventh antechamber, we no longer referred to being a person at peace but a peacemaker (Matthew 5:9, NKJV). What did Christ do as a true peacemaker? He bore our burdens (Matthew 11:28, NKJV). We must do the same. In other words, we must let others come to us.

Do you want to be a happy person? Go through the seven antechambers and you will find the happiness you were created for, even when others attack you; even when others curse you, you will be happy.

Chapter 15

---❖---

Peace in the Life
of the Believer

In this chapter, we will delve deeper into some practical aspects related to our main purpose in this world: that of being peacemakers, as we discovered in the seventh antechamber. Only when we create peace around us will we be called the sons and daughters of God.

You may have heard expressions like, "Like father, like son!" or "Like mother, like daughter!" Looking at God as our Father, we must become aware that we bear His image and are called to reflect His character. An ancient Romanian proverb, also present in the culture of the ancient Jews, says, "Every tree is known by its fruit." In the Gospel of Matthew, chapter 7, it is written that people do not gather grapes from thornbushes or figs from thistles (Matthew 7:16, NKJV). In the same way, the fruits of our lives must be evident: *"Even so, every good tree bears good fruit, but a bad tree bears bad fruit. A good tree*

*cannot bear bad fruit, nor can a bad tree bear good fruit...
Therefore by their fruits you will know them" (Matthew 7:17-
20, NKJV).*

**Are you a person of peace?
Is God's character visible in you,
or do you transform from a believer
into an uncontrolled person
when faced with difficulties?**

Why are there so many wars? Why do conflicts and tensions continue to exist in the world, between individuals, political parties, societies, and generations? Although the causes of these conflicts are complex, part of the problem may be that the fundamental principles of peace – such as self-denial, reconciliation, and unconditional love – are often misunderstood or misapplied.

Let us consider three basic principles that must be applied diligently and consistently every day in order to truly be people of peace.

Self-Denial: One of the first things we must learn on our spiritual journey is the willingness to give up certain personal rights or privileges for the good of others. When we model our character according to the teachings of God's Word, we understand that pride and prejudices must be set aside, and others must be seen as more important than ourselves. Moses experienced this principle when he encountered divine kind-ness and forgiveness, learning that self-denial and compas-sionate actions reflect an authentic relationship with God[96].

As we have learned, God shows us in Exodus 34 that His essence is forgiveness and self-sacrifice. He was willing to pay the ultimate price for our mistakes, even though He had com-mitted none. Even when people reject Him, He takes the first step toward reconciliation. In our lives, this divine model of self-denial must inspire us to sacrifice our own comfort and rights to uplift those around us, even if they offer us nothing in return.

Self-denial is not a sign of weakness, but a manifestation of inner strength and profound love. It is a call to reflect God's character through mercy, compassion, and empathy.

When we are willing to put ourselves second for the good of others, we take an essential step in becoming true peace-makers.

Pursuing Reconciliation: Address problems with the intention of bringing peace, not war! In the face of conflicts, it may be tempting to react with hostility or to avoid the issue

---

[96] Dietrich Bonhoeffer, *The Cost of Discipleship* (SCM Press, 2015), p. 87.

entirely, but our true calling is to be active peacemakers. This means seeking solutions that bring healing, not deepening wounds. When faced with a problem, we must ask ourselves: "How can I bring peace to this situation?" It is not enough to ignore conflicts or hide them; we must be willing to address them directly, with the goal of restoring harmony. The Bible teaches us, *"If your enemy is hungry, give him bread to eat; and if he is thirsty, give him water to drink" (Romans 12:20, NKJV).*

This approach is not about humiliating the other person, but about awakening their conscience and offering an opportunity for reconciliation. Only those with a strong and stable character can respond to evil with good, without seeking revenge. Bringing peace means becoming an agent of reconciliation, someone who does not avoid problems, but addresses them with love and a sincere desire to heal relationships. This way of living is not a sign of weakness, but of an inner strength that reflects the wisdom and gentleness of Christ[97].

Unconditional Love for Enemies: One of the most challenging teachings of Christ is the call to love our enemies. It is easy to love those who love us, but the true test of Christian love is the ability to love those who reject us or do us harm. This love is not conditioned by how we are treated, but is the result of a conscious choice to reflect God's love in all our relationships. Many people have a negative or defensive attitude because deep down, they long for more love and acceptance.

---

[97] Ken Sande, *The Peacemaker: A Biblical Guide to Resolving Personal Conflict* (Baker Books, 2004).

Our response must be to offer them this love, even if they do not ask for or deserve it. *"Be kindly affectionate to one another with brotherly love, in honour giving preference to one another" (Romans 12:10, NKJV).*

This is our calling – to see others as more important than ourselves, just as God did when He sent His Son among us[98].

Christ did not wait for us to change before loving us; He came and showed us His unconditional love.
We are called to do the same.

Love unconditionally, seek peace, and live in harmony with all people, as much as depends on us (Romans 12:18, NKJV). This love and desire to live in peace are what overcome evil and bring light into darkness.

These three principles – self-denial, addressing problems with the intention of bringing peace, and unconditional love for enemies – are essential for becoming true peacemakers. By applying them, we align ourselves with God's character and become ambassadors of peace in this world. It is not an easy path, but it is one that brings true happiness and spiritual fulfilment. Through our example, we can positively influence those around us and spread divine peace in our communities.

---

[98] C.S. Lewis, *The Four Loves* (Harperone, 2017).

On the foundation of these three principles, we will develop **ten essential behaviours** – daily practices without which it will be impossible for us to be peacemakers or bringers of peace:

1. Acknowledge Problems and Do Not Ignore Them

Often, we enter into conflict because we refuse to acknowledge the existence of problems. Sometimes, out of misunderstanding or fear, we choose to deny them, ignoring the fact that problems exist to be solved, not hidden. It is essential to learn to identify and accept their existence, no matter how uncomfortable they may be. The problem may have roots within yourself, reflecting how your character has been shaped or influenced by your experiences. These difficulties can interfere with those of others, creating conflicts. Until you address the problem with the intention of resolving it, the situation will not improve.

The Bible provides us with an important perspective in Jeremiah 6:13-14 (NKJV): *"Because from the least of them even to the greatest of them, everyone is given to covetousness; and from the prophet even to the priest, everyone deals falsely. They have also healed the hurt of My people slightly, saying, 'Peace, peace!' when there is no peace"*. This passage emphasises that pursuing peace does not mean hiding the reality of conflict and pretending everything is fine. True peace comes only when we are willing to confront and resolve real problems.

We often fail because we pretend everything is in order while malice, resentment, and desires for revenge persist in our hearts. To truly bring peace, we must identify the source of the problems, acknowledge them, and take action to resolve them. Temporary truces will never create lasting peace; they offer only a fleeting illusion of calm[99].

2. Resolve Conflicts as Soon as Possible

Do not let a conflict persist or escalate. What seems like an innocent spark today can tomorrow become an unquench-able fire that is capable of consuming your life. If you do not intervene in time, you may find yourself in a situation where the resources needed to extinguish this conflict are no longer sufficient.

To prevent such situations, it is essential to constantly develop Christian character traits. Without this preparation, you will not have the necessary mindset to react appropriately. Being a person of peace requires going through a process of spiritual and mental refinement. The lessons learned along the way will help you become a true emissary of peace, preventing the amplification of conflicts and protecting your relationships from the destruction caused by misunderstandings.

3. Develop Self-Control

Control your words, for the tongue can often be the sharp-est weapon—it can wound more deeply than any sword. As it is

---

[99] Ken Sande, *The Peacemaker: A Biblical Guide to Resolving Personal Conflict* (Grand Rapids, MI: Baker Books, 2004), p. 45.

written in James 1:19 (NKJV), *"So then, my beloved brethren, let every man be swift to hear, slow to speak, slow to wrath"*, we are encouraged to be mindful of how we express ourselves. In contemporary culture, there is a tendency to impose opinions forcefully, often hurting those who think differently. The Bible teaches us to speak *"with grace, seasoned with salt"* so that we know how to respond to everyone (Colossians 4:6, NKJV). This means our words should be well-thought-out and full of wisdom.

The concept of "salt" is borrowed from the culture of the ancient Jews, where salt symbolised the covenant between God and man (Leviticus 2:13, NKJV). Therefore, our speech should reflect this covenant, always being filled with kindness and respect. If we are part of this covenant, we will know how to respond to each person and how to face challenges.

We are created in the image and likeness of God, and as such, we are called to reflect this divine character in everything we do, including our speech. However, we often fail to control our words. Why? Because we forget who we are and what our faith represents.

Ion Luca Caragiale observed this tendency to express opinions without restraint in a text from 1897, noting that people come to believe that expressing an opinion is not only a right but an absolute duty: *"Expressing my opinion is the most sacred right I have as an individual thinker among my fellow men [...]. The king of creation, having succeeded in regaining his sceptre, exercises it with such deep conviction that he eventually believes his right is, in fact, a duty."*[100].

In the British Parliament, there is a rule of addressing "the honourable opponent," which requires respect for the person you are debating, even if their ideas are completely different. Thus, the person takes precedence, not the idea itself. Unfortunately, in modern society, the focus has shifted from the content of ideas to personal attacks, which destroy mutual respect. When we do not like others' ideas, we are tempted to attack the person directly, believing this will give more authority to our arguments. This is wrong and selfish behaviour.

We should not be like this; instead, we must develop the ability to control our speech. We must maintain spiritual balance. As Matthew 7:12 (NKJV) teaches us: *"Therefore, whatever you want men to do to you, do also to them"*. If we desire respect, we must first offer it. It all begins with self-control—with restraining our speech when the instinct is to hurt. Instead of seeing others as enemies, we must view them as our fellow human beings, deserving of respect and kindness, even if they disagree with us.

4. Prepare for a Spiritual Endurance Race

To become a true peacemaker, perseverance is necessary—a quality that is difficult to develop in a world full of conflicts and divergent interests. Perseverance requires strong spiritual endurance, capable of withstanding ongoing challenges. The Bible exhorts us: *"He who would love life and see good*

---

[100] *Epoca*, III, nr. 353, January 17, 1897.

days, let him refrain his tongue from evil, and his lips from speaking deceit. Let him turn away from evil and do good; let him seek peace and pursue it" (1 Peter 3:10-11, NKJV). This verse emphasises the importance of self-control, and a life dedicated to peace.

To become a person of peace, you must constantly work on your character. Transform yourself from a person prone to conflicts into a peacemaker. From someone ready to explode in anger, transform into a person who is tolerant, kind, and attentive—someone whose very presence brings peace, tranquillity, and comfort to those around them[101].

This transformation requires endurance. You will need diligence, vigilance, and education. If you wish to become a true peacemaker, you must cultivate discipline and willpower and rely on God. Without divine help, these qualities cannot be fully developed.

To have the power and resilience needed in this spiritual endurance race, it is essential to allow yourself to be shaped. The lessons from the previous six antechambers were just preparation. Now, in the seventh antechamber, you have the opportunity to apply everything you have learned and become the person you were meant to be.

---

[101] The Arbinger Institute, *The Anatomy of Peace: Resolving the Heart of Conflict* (San Francisco, CA: Berrett-Koehler Publishers, 2006), p. 35.

5. Aim for True Peace, Not Just Truces

Truces are easy to achieve, often based on temporary compromises. However, they do not resolve the problem in depth. Instead of addressing the bitterness and resentment that remain, the truce merely masks the conflict temporarily. Instead of settling for a truce, you must take the first step towards true peace. This requires courage—the courage to let go of pride and seek deep reconciliation. *"Be kindly affectionate to one another with brotherly love, in honour giving preference to one another... If it is possible, as much as depends on you, live peaceably with all men" (Romans 12:10, 18, NKJV).*

True peace does not just mean the absence of conflict; it requires complete disarmament—not just physical, but also mental and emotional.

Therefore, be a person of courage. Do not settle for temporary solutions to problems but pursue deep and lasting peace. This does not only mean reducing the means of conflict, but also renouncing destructive thoughts, the desire to hurt the other person, and any actions that could affect your fellow's well-being.

True peace means being willing to give up your own righteousness, to yield, to love, and to sacrifice for the good of the other. This is not easy to achieve and can only be learned through perseverance, self-control, morality, and spiritual maturity. Only by cultivating these qualities can you attain true peace—not just in your relationships, but also in your soul.[102]

6. Cultivate Mercy Through Empathy

Do not limit yourself to sympathy, and do not humiliate your adversary; instead, show deep mercy born out of empathy. True peace does not come from temporary compromises or superficial truces, but from a profound understanding of others' sufferings and needs.

The Scripture urges us to have the same attitude as Christ Jesus: *"Let this mind be in you which was also in Christ Jesus, who, being in the form of God, did not consider it robbery to be equal with God, but made Himself of no reputation, taking the form of a bondservant, and coming in the likeness of men. And being found in appearance as a man, He humbled Himself and became obedient to the point of death, even the death of the cross" (Philippians 2:5-8, NKJV).*

For the Jews, death on a tree was considered the ultimate curse (Deuteronomy 21:23; Galatians 3:13, NKJV). Yet, Christ accepted this curse for us—not out of obligation, but out of deep mercy and boundless empathy for our suffering. He was moved by our pain and rejoiced in our joy. He did not look down on us as mere pawns on a chessboard but as His brothers and sisters, His equals.

---

[102] Henri J.M. Nouwen, *The Way of the Heart: Connecting with God Through Prayer, Wisdom, and Silence* (New York, NY: Ballantine Books, 1981), p. 67.

God does not bring peace through force or power but through the victory of love and compassion. True empathy, which goes beyond temporary sympathies, is the key to lasting peace. When you love truly, you demonstrate divine authority; when you sacrifice for the good of another, you show supreme wisdom. Christ gave His life for us, renouncing all He had on earth to win us for eternity. And when He rose, He did so for us, to lead us to eternal glory.[103]

True peace is achieved through this deep mercy, which is born out of sincere empathy. It is the peace that not only transforms external circumstances, but also the hearts of people, thus bringing them closer to God and to one another.

7. Sacrifice for the Good of the Community

Devotion to God and His Church means more than mere participation; it involves a willingness to suffer for the well-being of others. As it is written: *"For this is commendable, if because of conscience toward God one endures grief, suffering wrongfully. For what credit is it if, when you are beaten for your faults, you take it patiently? But when you do good and suffer, if you take it patiently, this is commendable before God. For to this you were called, because Christ also suffered for us, leaving us an example, that you should follow His steps"* (1 Peter 2:19-21, NKJV).

Do not focus on your suffering or on temporary losses. How can you be a true person of peace if you feel defeated

---

[103] Dietrich Bonhoeffer, *The Cost of Discipleship* (New York, NY: Touchstone, 1995), p. 89.

when everything is taken from you? Remember that God paid the ultimate price, even for what He did not take. Why did He do it? Out of His deep love for us.

If you have learned what compassion is, you must know that it cannot exist without devotion. True love does not manifest itself only to obtain something in return; it is an expression of our divine nature. Being a person of peace does not mean seeking praise or recognition but acting from a deep nature of reconciliation and love for others.

Christ gave us the ultimate example of devotion: *"Who committed no sin, nor was deceit found in His mouth; who, when He was reviled, did not revile in return; when He suffered, He did not threaten, but committed Himself to Him who judges righteously; who Himself bore our sins in His own body on the tree, that we, having died to sins, might live for righteousness—by whose stripes you were healed" (1 Peter 2:22-24, NKJV).*

Thus, devotion means accepting personal loss and suffering, offering your life for the edification of the body of Christ—the Church.

———————• •———————

This is our calling: to live not for ourselves but for others, in the name of divine love.

———————• •———————

8. Pray for Peace

Praying for peace is not just a personal act of devotion, but also an active contribution to the harmony and stability of the world. Psalm 122:6 (NKJV) exhorts us: *"Pray for the peace of Jerusalem: May they prosper who love you"*. This prayer is not merely a request; it is also a promise and a blessing for you and for me. Through this verse, we are encouraged to be consistent in our actions, to persevere in reaching our goals, and to remain attentive to the directions God gives us.

Jerusalem, called the "city of peace," symbolises divine harmony. However, throughout history, this city has been a point of tension and conflict. Why? Because true peace is difficult to achieve and is often undermined by forces that oppose God's plan. In a turbulent world, in the midst of the storm, we all try to navigate to the shores of safety and peace. This storm is fuelled by the forces of evil that seek to disrupt divine harmony. Jerusalem is meant to be the source from which peace flows to the entire world. Therefore, your prayer for peace is not just a simple devotion; it is a spiritual weapon against the evil that tries to disrupt divine harmony. Remember that prayer must be supported by diligence and perseverance. Confront any instinct to react violently or to harm, knowing that true peace comes from a heart devoted to prayer and loving action.

9. Spread the Good News of Peace

Be an ambassador of peace and reconciliation, carrying the message of the Gospel through deeds, not just through words. As Scripture exhorts us: *"and having shod your feet with the preparation of the gospel of peace" (Ephesians 6:15, NKJV)*.

———————•   •———————

In today's world, many use the Gospel as a tool for judgment and criticism. However, God calls us to be healers, not accusers. He desires for us to bring healing, deliverance, harmony, and understanding—not division or malice.

———————•   •———————

Be a bearer of God's image. Spread the Gospel of peace through every action and decision you make. Be a living example of how to live a life of peace and love, so that others see in you a true child of God. Be an emissary of peace, allowing those around you to see that your life is a continuous manifestation of Christ's message.

Through your example, show others that the Gospel is not just a message, but a call to a life of reconciliation, kindness, and love. In a world often marked by conflicts and misunderstandings, be the light that brings God's peace into the hearts and lives of those you encounter. This means always being ready to spread the message of peace and to work for harmony in all relationships.

10. Cultivate Peace When You Have Found It

Do not be content simply with having found peace; do not leave it in an early state. Cultivate it, help it flourish, and bring fruit into your life and the lives of those around you. True peace requires constant attention and care. Adopt a proactive attitude, focused on developing this state of peace, keeping it alive and vibrant in all aspects of your life.

Strive to keep the unity of the Spirit through the bond of peace. Do not stop at the first step, thinking you are already complete. On the contrary, continue to practice peace every day, in all your interactions. Make peace a way of life, a natural reflex in all your relationships and decisions.

Let peace be visible in your life. Seek daily opportunities to practice it, promote it, and create alliances with others who share the same desire for harmony. Surround yourself with friends who share this vision and discuss how you can maintain peace in your hearts and in your community.

Do not stop at a personal level. Help others find their peace. Be a pillar of support for those who still have inner or outer conflicts. Create a strategy for yourself today and a model for living in peace tomorrow. Practice this consistently in your life, and you will find that true happiness comes from a heart full of peace.

Act using a long-term perspective. Prepare yourself for the moments when the storm knocks at your door, and do not let the opportunities to bring peace go unnoticed.

As we reach the exit from the seventh antechamber, we understand what it truly means to be children of God and to live a life full of happiness—a life of makarios. We have learned what it means to be people of value in a world full of shadows, to be more than mere bearers of the divine character.

We have realised that without God's help, our powers are limited and that only with Him can we advance in life. We have discovered that pride and prejudice can bring us down, but a divine mindset centred on God will make us flourish. We have learned to guard ourselves from sin and to be aware of the true nature of temptations so that we can drive them out of our lives. We have learned to be humble, to hunger and thirst for righteousness, to be merciful, to have a pure heart, and to practice peace. The peace of God, which surpasses all human understanding, transforms our minds and our daily behaviour.

To become such a person, it is essential to learn to recognise the problems in your life and face them with courage. Be cautious and resolve conflicts and problems quickly before they escalate. Develop self-control—especially the ability to hold your tongue. Prepare for a spiritual endurance race; it will not be easy, but with spiritual balance, you will succeed. Take the first step towards true peace, not just temporary truces. Seek peace that springs from deep empathy, not mere sympathy. Accept the personal loss and suffering in exchange for building the body of Christ. Pray. Preach the Gospel and bear fruit.

By doing all these things, you will become a fulfilled Christian in this world—a person who reflects God. You may expect others to bring you praise and admire you. But know that once you step out of this final antechamber and re-enter life, after having learned what it means to be a happy person, you will see the world with new eyes. You will understand that true happiness does not come from the praises or approval of others, but from the deep and lasting peace you have cultivated in your heart, reflecting God in everything you do.

Chapter 16

---◆---

The Silence of the Lambs

"Blessed are those who are persecuted
for righteousness' sake,
for theirs is the kingdom of heaven"
Matthew 5:10 (NKJV).

When we embarked on the path of rediscovering happiness and realised that refining our character is the foundation of true joy, we understood that we must give up many habits and behaviours that kept us captive in life without perspective. These habits condemned us to the routine of an unfulfilled existence, making us prisoners of societal norms.

Once we take a stand and make determined steps toward change, we will inevitably face opposition from those around us. Think of our new mindset as a bright light that stands out in a sea of darkness, contrasting with what others consider acceptable. This change can provoke hostility, being perceived as a threat to their way of life. In our presence, those trapped in a limited, joyless existence, will feel insecure. Some will react out of jealousy, others out of envy, while others will simply not understand the transformation taking place within us.

We live in a profoundly corrupt society where being righteous, kind, and authentic can become uncomfortable for those around us. In a world dominated by conflicts and selfishness, living according to moral values is a constant challenge. Our Savior Jesus Christ warned us long ago about this reality: *"Behold, I send you out as sheep in the midst of wolves. Therefore be wise as serpents and harmless as doves" (Matthew 10:16, NKJV)*. The image of a sheep among wolves perfectly reflects the contrast between those who choose the path of righteousness and those who live in the chaos of the world.

However, being harmless does not mean being naive. Adapted to the context of today's society, the wisdom of serpents involves diplomacy and discernment.

Perhaps you already feel that you are on dangerous ground in this world, where people seem more like enemies than friends. Nevertheless, you can positively influence those around you through diplomacy, kindness, and righteousness. You can even lead them to reevaluate their own attitudes and behaviours. Be a person without malice, but not without wisdom.

———• •———

Kindness should not be confused with weakness; it must be supported by firmness rooted in wisdom.

———• •———

You should not be surprised when you encounter opposition from those around you. After tasting the happiness that comes from living according to moral values, you will also experience the bitterness that accompanies this change. It is inevitable. When you choose to live in truth and righteousness, this choice becomes a bright light in a dense darkness. Those accustomed to their old way of life will perceive this light as a threat, a disturbance of their comfort.

The title of this chapter, "The Silence of the Lambs," evokes the image of a delicate transition between two distinct worlds. We have left behind an existence where we were prisoners of norms and habits that did not bring happiness, but we have not yet fully arrived in the "promised land," where "milk and honey flow." In this transitional period, like lambs standing silent in the face of change, we find ourselves in a place of uncertainty and reflection. The silence of the lambs symbolises a dignified and calm gentleness in the face of oppression and inevitable changes, representing the moment of lying in wait and contemplation and preparing for what is to come. Although the price of happiness may seem high at this intermediate point, it is a price truly worth paying.

Corruption is entrenched in every aspect of our society and being a righteous person that exudes kindness and truth becomes uncomfortable for those around us. Therefore, we must be prepared for opposition. But we must not despair. God is not cruel. When He allows us to taste from this fruit of bitterness, it is to refine our character and to help us see the world as it truly is.[104]

The essential question is: What should we do in such a situation? First of all, we must remember that the Savior warned us that we would be persecuted for our righteousness. In Matthew 5:10 (NKJV), He tells us: *"Blessed are those who are persecuted for righteousness' sake, for theirs is the kingdom of heaven"*. If you choose to live according to moral values, you should not expect applause or praise from those around you. We live in a world that, economically and socially speaking, favours conflict and war, not peace. However, we are called to promote and practice peace, even when the world around us does not desire it.

The persecution that Jesus speaks of happens "for righteousness' sake," a term that in Greek means "justice." To be a person of righteousness means to be honest, to not lie, to not pretend, and to not perform charitable acts just to draw attention to oneself.

———————————• •———————————

God does not need appearances but authenticity. He does not want us to display

---

[104] A.W. Tozer, *The Pursuit of God* (Chicago: Moody Publishers, 1982).

*our good deeds, but to do them from a
pure heart, without seeking rewards or
recognition from people.*

———————• •———————

A biblical example of a righteous person is Elijah, who thought he was the only one left in Israel, facing oppression and difficulties. However, God revealed to him that He had reserved seven thousand others who were just as righteous as he was (1 Kings 19:10-18). Similarly, even when we feel isolated or persecuted for living according to righteous principles, we must remember that we are not alone in this fight. Therefore, let us love righteousness, not for personal fame, but because this is the path God desires for us.

Blessed are those who are persecuted for righteousness, for theirs is the kingdom of heaven. To reach this status, we need to go through all the steps previously discussed. Everything begins with recognising our own powerlessness: *"Blessed are the poor in spirit, for theirs is the kingdom of heaven" (Matthew 5:3, NKJV).* This is the first step on the path of righteousness: recognising personal failure. When you do this, you begin to detach from unrighteousness and love righteousness. And when you love righteousness, you will discover that it is not always easy to follow. Since they are accustomed to living in compromises and lies, those around you will be disturbed by the light you bring into their lives.

The Savior warns us that true happiness does not come without costs: *"Blessed are you when they revile and persecute you, and say all kinds of evil against you falsely for My sake"* *(Matthew 5:11, NKJV)*. This persecution is not just a simple misunderstanding, but a manifestation of malice that uses untruth to affect your identity. People will spread lies about you to discredit you. But you should not be discouraged by these attacks. Remember that those who attack you are also seeking love and acceptance. Sometimes, those who attack you can become friends if they get to know you better.

How should you react when you are persecuted? The Lord Jesus teaches us: *"Rejoice and be exceedingly glad, for great is your reward in heaven" (Matthew 5:12, NKJV)*. You should not expect recognition or rewards here on earth. Your persecution will be rewarded in heaven, where your reward is eternal. In this life, you may not receive recognition from those around you. But what truly matters is the perspective of eternity, where true happiness and reward await you.[105]

When you are truly persecuted for righteousness, you know that you have made decisions in accordance with God's will and followed the path of righteousness. This is the path of authentic happiness, even though it is not easy. True persecution comes when you live a life that reflects divine values, and the opposition of the world only confirms that you are on the right path.

——————————• •——————————

The conclusion is clear: persecution for righteousness is part of our spiritual

---

[105] Dietrich Bonhoeffer, *The Cost of Discipleship* (New York: Simon & Schuster, 1995).

journey. It is proof of our faith and our commitment to God.

———————• •———————

The happiness we are promised in the Gospels is not obtained without struggle, but the reward is far greater than any momentary suffering. God calls us to remain faithful even in the face of difficulties, knowing that the kingdom of heaven awaits us.

Thus, when you face persecution, remember that you are not alone. Many others have walked the same path before you, and their reward is already prepared. Be courageous, remain faithful to divine principles, and look ahead with hope. This is the path of authentic happiness, which is not based on the recognition of the world, but on the eternal promises of God.

To truly suffer for Christ, you must have gone through a profound spiritual process, symbolised by the seven antechambers—a journey of spiritual maturity and soul purification. Otherwise, your suffering might have nothing to do with faith and may actually be the result of your own actions or wrong decisions.

According to the Oxford English Dictionary, persecution is defined as the systematic and sustained harassment or oppression of an individual or group, especially on the grounds of their race, religion, or political beliefs, often carried out by those in positions of power with the intent to subjugate or harm. In practice, persecution involves a deliberate and systematic action meant to destroy or cause intentional suffering. Conversely, harassment refers to an unjust and continuous pursuit of a person, not necessarily from a position of authority and without the explicit intention of destroying them, but rather causing harm or inconvenience.

Therefore, we must be vigilant and constantly examine our behaviour, especially if we have authority over others. Pastors, preachers, and religious leaders must be extremely careful not to end up persecuting their flock, either through direct acts or by omission.

Persecution and harassment can manifest in two major areas: physical violence and verbal violence. We know well that verbal violence can sometimes be more painful than physical violence. Words have the power to wound deeply, and the wounds they cause are much harder to heal. How many times have we heard people say, "I'd rather have been slapped than hear those words"? This deep pain, born from verbal attacks, can be devastating to the soul.

If you intend to be an authentic believer, be prepared to be struck, both physically and verbally. This is the reality of a life of faith in a world that does not easily accept the light. But you should not be surprised or discouraged by this.

The purpose is not to hide from suffering but to face it with dignity and find in it a deeper meaning. God does not promise us an easy

road, but He gives us the strength to pass through trials.[106]

———————• •———————

You may wonder why believers are persecuted. Why did God not prepare for us a smooth road, paved with gold and precious stones, that we could walk on without worries? The answer to this question requires a profound understanding of the contemporary life of faith. Today, we often hear preached a "prosperity Gospel", which promises believers material success, perfect relationships, and constant appreciation from those around them. However, this idyllic image does not reflect reality. When you try to do good, you will quickly discover that you do not always receive gratitude. Instead, you may face opposition and rejection.

It is essential therefore to understand that your suffering is not always the result of your mistakes. In a world where good is often perceived as a threat, those who desire to live in truth and righteousness will attract the attention of those who prefer darkness. This is a harsh reality, but also proof of authentic faith, as illustrated in Philippians 1:29-30 (NKJV): *"For to you it has been granted on behalf of Christ, not only to believe in Him, but also to suffer for His sake, having the same conflict which you saw in me and now hear is in me."*

The life of faith is not a path covered in roses. The apostle Paul boasted about those believers who demonstrated their

---

[106] Lewis, C.S. *The Problem of Pain.* HarperOne, 2001.

faith through *"all their persecutions and tribulations that you endure"* (2 Thessalonians 1:4, NKJV).

God allows these trials not to destroy us but to purify and perfect our character.

He expects us to react differently from the world, even in the face of suffering. That is why Peter encourages us: *"Beloved, do not think it strange concerning the fiery trial which is to try you, as though some strange thing happened to you; but rejoice to the extent that you partake of Christ's sufferings, that when His glory is revealed, you may also be glad with exceeding joy. If you are reproached for the name of Christ, blessed are you, for the Spirit of glory and of God rests upon you"* (1 Peter 4:12-14, NKJV).

The Spirit of God, also called the "Spirit of glory," rests upon those who are reproached for the name of Christ. In Hebrew culture, the term "Kabod" designates the glory of God, often associated with the idea of spiritual weight or importance, symbolising divine greatness and dignity. This "weight" is not physical, but represents the invaluable value and honour brought by the presence of God.

When the Spirit of glory rests upon you, it means that your life reflects the presence and character of God. Your relationship with God becomes so profound that people around you can see His manifestation in you. This is one of the main reasons why the world may react in a hostile manner. Those attached to evil cannot bear the light of truth and righteousness; when you reflect God's image, your presence can trigger this opposition.

Scripture tells us that people had a different preference: *"And this is the condemnation, that the light has come into the world, and men loved darkness rather than light, because their deeds were evil. For everyone practicing evil hates the light and does not come to the light, lest his deeds should be exposed. But he who does the truth comes to the light, that his deeds may be clearly seen, that they have been done in God"* *(John 3:19-21, NKJV).*

There is a universal pattern of persecution, seen in the opposition that an authentic believer feels from the world. It is an experience you must face daily because, first and foremost, light is a disturbance. As long as you remain in God's presence, the world may reject you, not because of who you are, but because His presence is reflected in you, and those who live in darkness cannot endure the light.

This opposition is not new. From the beginning of human history, righteous people have been persecuted by those who lived in darkness. Cain killed Abel because Abel's offering was accepted by God, while his own was not. Joseph was thrown into prison because he chose to live righteously. Moses was criticised and rejected by his own people, even by his sister and brother, for following God's plans. Do you remember Elijah? He was hunted and persecuted all his life, ending up eating the crumbs brought by ravens. Nehemiah was defamed and slandered. Stephen was stoned to death. Peter and John were thrown into prison. Paul and Silas ended up with their feet in stocks. James was beheaded.

The entire work of our forebears is a chapter of the persecution, defamation, and humiliation of those who sincerely loved God. From our own age, we remember people like Traian Dorz, Nicolae Moldoveanu, Richard Wurmbrand, and Iosif Ţon.

All of them were persecuted, struck, and beaten for one ideal: to love God publicly, not just in secret.

And it was not only the authorities who persecuted them; the blows often came from friends and even brothers in faith.

A corrupt world will often use those closest to you to subtly strike you and try to bring you down rather than to create a person of faith and holiness. The most painful blow often comes from those closest to you—your spouse, children, grandchildren, brothers, and sisters in faith. It is easier for us to tolerate the words and attacks of those we do not know. But it is infinitely harder when these attacks come from those we love! Throughout history, there have been torturers who infiltrated good people, taking the form of the best and most devoted friends until the prey was easy to strike down.

Remember that Satan acts from within. Just as wolves infiltrate the sheepfold to attack them, Satan has placed his followers among the believers, knowing that the pain and impact are much greater when the blow comes from within the flock. This subtle tactic shows that the most painful betrayals do not often come from outside, but from those in whom we had the most trust.

How many unknown people have insulted you directly, calling you a bad, proud, arrogant, unbeliever, and worldly person? On the other hand, how many of your brothers and sisters have told you the same things, and this has hurt you on a deeper level?

The light of Christ shining in us will always attract persecution from the world. Like a beacon in the night, we will attract insects and creatures that will try to spit on us and darken our rays of light. Similarly, when you shine, be aware that you will be surrounded by people, but also by the spirits of wickedness that will try to sting and mock you. But we should not fear, for Jesus Christ has already warned us that these attacks are an inevitable part of the life of faith: *"If they persecuted Me, they will also persecute you. If they kept My word, they will keep yours also. But all these things they will do to you for My name's sake, because they do not know Him who sent Me"* *(John 15:20-21, NKJV)*. The apostle Paul concludes: *"Yes, and all who desire to live godly in Christ Jesus will suffer persecution. But evil men and impostors will grow worse and worse, deceiving and being deceived" (2 Timothy 3:12-13, NKJV).*

Thus, persecution is a sign of authentic faith. I ask you: Have you ever been persecuted? Have you been harassed because of your faith? If yes, good on you! If you have not yet experienced this, prepare yourself, for it will come for you too. Persecution is a sign of authentic faith. If you have not yet been persecuted for your faith, it does not mean you will not be. It is only a matter of time. Authentic faith attracts opposition, but also the blessing of God.

───────── • • ─────────

Persecution is a part of our journey to heaven. It is not just a test, but also a means through which God shapes our character, purifies our faith, and prepares us for eternity.

───────── • • ─────────

We must trust in Him, knowing that, as the Lord Jesus said in Matthew 10:16 (NKJV), *"I send you out as sheep in the midst of wolves,"* we are sent to fulfil a divine purpose through our perseverance in the face of sufferings. Thus, the path of faith is not easy, but full of meaning and purpose. In the midst of our suffering, we must remember that we are not alone. God is with us, and His light shines through us even in the darkest moments.

Returning to the essential question of this chapter: Does God want to see us suffer? Is persecution a necessary element in the life of a believer, with both positive and negative values, or only negative ones? Once we choose to follow God, must we only prepare for blows and suffering?

Persecution does not come from God's desire to torment or mock us. God does not wish us harm; He knows our weaknesses. Often, as humans, we forget quickly, fall prey to temptations, and exceed the limits of faith. The apostle Paul urges us to persist in faith, reminding us that *"we must through many tribulations enter the kingdom of God" (Acts 14:22, NKJV).* These tribulations are not gratuitous punishment, but a consequence of life in a world that often opposes divine values. Persecution purifies the Church and separates authentic believers from those who only pretend to be faithful.[107]

At one point, the Savior made a meaningful statement: *"I am the door. If anyone enters by Me, he will be saved, and will go in and out and find pasture" (John 10:9, NKJV).* You may say that, for you, this door is often so narrow that you can barely squeeze through! When you pass through it, you begin to feel how every inch of yourself gets scratched, and you wonder why God does not make your life easy, since you can see others having it easier. What you do not realise at that moment is that the narrow and rough doorposts you have passed through, and which have scraped your body, soul, and mind, managed to catch all those ugly parasites that have attached themselves to you over time, and which you sometimes didn't even notice.

---

[107] Ehrman, Bart D. *God's Problem: How the Bible Fails to Answer Our Most Important Question – Why We Suffer.* HarperOne, 2008.

Like greedy leeches, these things were draining your energy, and you accepted them as part of your life.

Therefore, do not complain
about the trials you are going through,
but thank God for refining your character
and for helping you remove the impurities
that pull you back.

In a world full of challenges, how can we recognise who our true brothers in faith are? A person who truly knows God will love you unconditionally, regardless of your imperfections and mistakes. An authentic believer will not seek to judge or persecute you for the unwise words you might speak. In contrast, those who have not experienced the true love of God tend to become persecutors. These are the people who will always have something to say and will not rest until they express their opinion. Their speech reveals their character, and their reactions expose them for who they truly are.

Persecution can take many forms. Sometimes, it is evident, manifesting through physical or verbal violence. Other times, persecution is subtle and insidious, appearing in the form of temptation or worldly pleasures. This "white persecution" can be just as dangerous, as it can lead you away from the right path without you even realising it. Expressions like *"God loves you as you are"* or *"You do not need to do more"* may sound comforting, but they can hide a dangerous trap. They can lead to complacency and spiritual stagnation, gradually moving you away from the sacrifice and dedication required by true faith.[108]

In the face of trials and persecution, we must keep our faith and understand that God calls us to a life of holiness and sacrifice.

If we pass through the valley of the shadow of death, we must do so with the conviction that these trials will make us spiritually stronger and draw us closer to God.

Christian diplomacy does not mean aggressive reactions, but wise and gentle responses, even when we are struck: *"Therefore be wise as serpents and harmless as doves" (Matthew 10:16, NKJV).* Wisdom urges us to respond to challenges with diplomacy, to be mindful of our words and actions, without provoking war.

Although people may strike us, our goal is not to reject them or to get revenge them, but to win them for Christ. They might seem to be our enemies today, but these people are valuable in God's eyes. If we win them for Him, we will gain a

---

[108] Kinnaman, David, and Mark Matlock. *Faith for Exiles: 5 Ways for a New Generation to Follow Jesus in Digital Babylon.* Baker Books, 2019.

great treasure. Every one of our reactions must be guided by the desire to bring light and hope, not conflict and destruction.

An example of a wise reaction is seen in the Lord Jesus. When He was led to slaughter, He did not open His mouth to defend or retaliate, but responded with silence and compassion (Isaiah 53:7, NKJV). This silence was not a sign of resignation but a divine strategy to win the spiritual battle. Our calling is to imitate this reaction of the Lord Jesus, recognising the value brought by silence, which reflects the gentle and transformative power of divine love.

Thus, our reaction in the face of persecution must be one of compassion and patience, even if we are provoked to war.

Scripture teaches us to have *"honourable conduct among the Gentiles, that when they speak against you as evildoers, they may, by your good works which they observe, glorify God in the day of visitation"* (1 Peter 2:12, NKJV). This good conduct can turn enemies into friends and, eventually, into brothers in faith. Our wisdom lies in responding to challenges with love and patience, not with revenge or resentment.

We cannot react correctly and do good deeds until we pass through the "seven antechambers" of spiritual formation.

Imagine that those who strike you are on a mountain crest, throwing stones at you, while you are on another crest. You have two options: to run further so that the stones do not reach you or to create a bridge of kindness towards them instead of moving away.

The biblical history of the Jewish people offers us numerous examples of how such a bridge of kindness can have unforeseen effects, even across generations. King David is a relevant example. When he was cursed and publicly mocked by Shimei, a member of King Saul's family, David chose not to punish him. Although his generals urged him to execute Shimei, David refused, demonstrating rare wisdom and compassion. This kindness had long-term consequences, allowing the continuation of Shimei's genealogical line, which led to the birth of Mordecai, a man who later saved the Jewish people from extermination during Queen Esther's time.

This example shows us that kindness and mercy can transform evil into good, even across generations. Imagine if David had ordered Shimei's execution—Mordecai, the saviour of the Jewish people, would not have existed.

But the story does not end there. The plot to exterminate the Jewish people was orchestrated by Haman, a descendant of Agag, king of the Amalekites, whom King Saul spared against God's command. If Saul had obeyed, Haman would not have existed, and his wickedness would not have threatened the Jewish people. This complex history teaches us that disobedience and lack of kindness can have devastating consequences, but God can turn evil into good when people choose to obey Him.

Where wickedness multiplies, God can multiply kindness to counter and nullify it. Kindness is a trait of those who have been refined for God. When the Spirit of God's glory rests upon you in the midst of persecution, you will produce the fruit of the Holy Spirit. According to Galatians 5:22 (NKJV), this fruit includes kindness, which is essential for facing persecution. Without kindness, you will be tempted to repay evil for evil. But when you are full of kindness, you will see those who strike you as your friends, and you will love them even more.

If you choose to live this way, you will become a true light in the world, an example of virtue that exudes kindness, right-eousness, and truth. When you are mocked, remember that God's blessing is upon you, for the Spirit of His glory rests on you. Be kind, even when it is difficult, and you will not only gain an unwavering mindset, but also the respect of those who once struck you. Through your attitude of love, you will demonstrate that true greatness comes from forgiveness and compassion.

If you are struck today, respond in love; if you are insult-ed, respond with kindness and "the silence of the lambs"; if you are persecuted, respond in self-sacrifice. Your graceful re-sponse will become a powerful testimony of your faith and of the transformative power of love.

Chapter 17

Victorious in Persecution

"If the world hates you,
you know that it hated Me
before it hated you [...];
but because you are not of the world,
but I chose you out of the world,
therefore the world hates you"
(John 15:18-19, NKJV).

According to the Oxford English Dictionary, a courageous person is someone who shows bravery, boldness, and determination, coupled with a wise approach. This is someone who plans each action with the aim of achieving a clear and well-defined objective. Courage does not just mean acting boldly, but also committing oneself to following a set path towards a specific goal. A Christian with such courage follows the example of the Saviour, who showed us the way in life, to gain *"the prize of the upward call of God" (Philippians 3:14, NKJV).*

In the previous chapter, we learned that when we strive to refine our character and live ethically and morally, society around us will not welcome us with open arms or applause. On the contrary, the light of truth shining through us will create discomfort for some people. They may feel threatened in our presence and, more often than not, choose to marginalise or persecute us.

This hostility comes from the same hatred with which the world rejected God. His light reveals hidden evil in actions and intentions, and those who live in darkness cannot bear this exposure. Therefore, they will hate us, just as they hated Him. What should we do when we are persecuted? We should view persecution as an opportunity to demonstrate an attitude that is worthy of a believer.

We return to the teaching from Matthew 10:16 (NKJV): *"Behold, I send you out as sheep in the midst of wolves. Therefore be wise as serpents and harmless as doves"*. Picture sheep entering the midst of a pack of wolves. They appear to be certain prey, an inevitable sacrifice. Yet, this sacred text teaches us that although we are vulnerable, we must be wise and gentle, prepared to win the hearts of those around us through innocent kindness.

Those who are persecuted for their moral and ethical principles can find the path to happiness if they choose not to see themselves as victims, but to act with wisdom and gentleness, positioning themselves wisely before their adversaries. Instead of being crushed by attacks, they can use discernment to gain respect and, perhaps, even the hearts of those who oppose them.

At the beginning of our journey, we discussed the relationship between our values and our daily behaviour. Our values and beliefs shape and continuously refine our character. If we analyse our daily actions, we can discover what values guide us and how they influence our character. For example, if we are led by deceit, malice, or if we seek validation from those who lack integrity, we are on the wrong path. This desire to use immoral means betrays the substance that has shaped our character. Even if the exterior appears pleasing, the inner reality will be bitter. Thus, our character—defined as the collection of fundamental traits—always reflects the values we have cultivated throughout life.

Our attitudes are expressions of our beliefs and subtle manifestations of how we perceive and influence the world. However, two people may share the same fundamental belief, yet express it differently through their attitudes, depending on their experiences, emotions, or social context. Therefore, we must be mindful of our attitudes, as good intentions can lead to harmful behaviour if we are not aware of the impact of our actions.[109]

For instance, when someone publicly corrects us in a humiliating way, it does not necessarily stem from a lack of moral values, but rather from a misunderstanding of how to apply those beliefs. Such behaviour may be the result of a cultural or social context that views public correction as an effective method for enforcing norms, even though it really causes more

---

[109] Sun, Key. "3 Reasons That Good Intentions May Lead to Bad Outcomes." *Psychology Today*, 2021.

harm than good. Therefore, we must recognise that applying a belief is influenced not only by the belief itself, but also by how we have learned to implement it in our relationships with others.

It is easy, then, to slip from
being persecuted to becoming
a persecutor, even when we believe
we are acting the right way.

Without deep reflection on our attitudes, we risk justifying destructive behaviour, mistakenly thinking it reflects our moral values.

A correct attitude does not seek to judge or expose the faults of others. It manifests love and kindness, even if that brings about reprisals. In Romans 12:9 (NKJV), we are told that love must be sincere and our relationships should be based on kindness and respect: *"Let love be without hypocrisy. Abhor what is evil. Cling to what is good".*

Our responsibility is not to correct others aggressively, but to love them with brotherly affection. This means giving them preference, sincerely enjoying their presence, and lifting them up, even when we feel they may not deserve it.

Regarding our relationships, Scripture urges us to follow the example of the Saviour, living in harmony with everyone, avoiding selfish ambitions, and maintaining an attitude of humility without considering ourselves wiser than others (Romans 12:11-16, NKJV). We are called to be devoted, to persevere patiently in the face of troubles, and to remain steadfast in prayer. We are also called to bless even those who persecute us.

When we are truly shaped
in the image of God,
we will not harshly
criticise our peers;
rather, we will bless and serve them,
leaving judgment to God.

"Repay no one evil for evil" (Romans 12:17, NKJV). Instead, we are called to always pursue what is good and peaceful. If we feel the need to correct someone, let us do so gently, not harshly, for we are all made of the same substance. Let us strive to uplift others, showing them kindness and nobility, just as we would wish to be treated.

Although painful, persecution can be transformed into a valuable opportunity for spiritual growth and character refinement. Looking more closely at the effects persecution has on us, we can identify four fundamental principles that can help us navigate these trials and emerge victorious.

1. Persecution Perfects Our Character

Persecution can be compared to an unpleasant alarm clock that forces us to wake up from spiritual slumber. However, as we understand the purpose of this "awakening," we end up being grateful for it.

Just as an alarm wakes us from physical sleep, persecution serves to rouse us from spiritual sleep and to help us develop patience. This patience leads to triumph, and triumph brings hope.

Every pain, every trouble is a tool in God's hands, that shapes and refines our character, much like a craftsman transforms a rough crystal into a sparkling diamond. Let us thank God for persecution, for it draws us closer to Him and offers us the opportunity to become stronger in faith. When we learn to be grateful for persecution, the pain lessens, and the trials become more bearable, transforming the valley of the shadow of death into a song of joy.

2. Persecution Shapes Our Speech and Relationships

Persecution also gives us the opportunity to discern between good and evil, both in our personal lives and in our relationships with others. For instance, our words can be powerful weapons—they can wound or heal, build up or tear down.

Through persecution, we learn to be more aware of the impact of our words on those around us. When we experience first-hand how painful thoughtless words can be, we learn to measure our words more carefully and to be more mindful of how we address others.

Our speech should be *"with grace, seasoned with salt"* *(Colossians 4:6, NKJV)*, so that we know how to answer to everyone and conduct ourselves with dignity even before those who persecute us. Thus, persecution not only shapes our patience, but also our speech, actions, and attitudes, helping us respond with kindness even in the face of hostility.

A person's true character is revealed in times of trial. Those who only have a superficial faith will give up, but those who are truly faithful will remain steadfast, being the "wheat" that God preserves.

However, before judging others, we must examine ourselves. Do our words and deeds reflect the faith we profess? It is easy to see the faults of others, but the real challenge is to examine our own actions and motives. Let us ensure we live according to the principles of Christ, for only in this way can we truly be worthy of being called children of God.

In the end, persecution not only purifies and refines us, but it also reveals our true nature. It is a test of our character, faith, and words. If we endure these trials with dignity and faith, we will come out stronger and closer to God. Though painful, persecution is a necessary process to remove the evil within us and to bring forth the goodness that God has sown in our hearts.

Why does all this happen? Because God has a well-defined plan for each of us and a reward proportionate to how we have fulfilled our mission on earth.

———————● ●———————

Persecution helps you eliminate the evil within you, so that goodness can shine through. When God allows trials in your life, it is not to destroy you, but to perfect you.

———————● ●———————

Instead of complaining about difficulties, learn to be grateful for them, for these are the tools through which God shapes you. Every trial you go through is an opportunity to become stronger, more resilient, and more faithful. Do not run away from God, and do not turn your back on Him during times of trial.

3. Persecution Contributes to Your Heavenly Treasure

The happiness promised to those who are persecuted is the kingdom of heaven (Matthew 5:10, NKJV). However, there is no egalitarianism in heaven, but rather a hierarchy based on merit: *"He who sows sparingly will also reap sparingly, and he who sows bountifully will also reap bountifully"* (2 Corinthians 9:6, NKJV). An illustrative parable is the one about the ten minas in the Gospel of Luke, chapter 19. This parable describes how ten servants received ten minas each to invest and bring profit to their master. At the end, each servant receives a reward proportionate to the results of his work. This parable underlines an essential truth: divine reward is proportionate to our deeds. The one who invested well receives authority over ten cities, while the one who worked less receives five cities. This reflects the fact that the reward in heaven is not distributed equally, but according to how much we have invested and worked for God. The one who took risks, who worked diligently, and kept his faith amidst persecution, will receive a greater reward.

This principle should motivate us to not flee from responsibilities and actions that might attract persecution. If we choose the path of comfort, if we avoid confrontation out of fear of suffering, we cannot expect great rewards. Do not hide from trials; embrace them, thanking God for the lessons you learn through them.

Amid trials and persecution, look confidently to the reward promised by God. Every sacrifice you make in His name, every suffering you endure, adds to your heavenly treasure. The path of faith is one of sacrifice, but also of eternal reward.

Be steadfast, remain faithful, and remember that *"the sufferings of this present time are not worthy to be compared with the glory which shall be revealed in us" (Romans 8:18, NKJV).* If you have not yet been persecuted, expect that persecution will come at the right time, for as it is written: *"If they persecuted Me, they will also persecute you" (John 15:20-21, NKJV)*. It is inevitable that those who live godly lives will be persecuted. In the meantime, make sure you maintain a proper attitude and live according to the principles of your faith.

Evil people will continue to do evil, but you remain peaceful, godly, and worthy of honour. Scripture urges us to be servants of Christ, faithful to what has been entrusted to us (1 Corinthians 4:1-2, NKJV). Fill your character with God's ethics and morality and spread the truth. But know that as soon as you begin to bear spiritual fruit, you will be attacked. Persecution is, and will remain, a constant for those who do good and live in truth.

To strengthen your character, remember those who are persecuted even now. Do not remain indifferent!

———————• •———————

Even if you are not yet in the midst of the fight, others may already be there.
Pray for them and offer your support, for in doing so, you prepare yourself for the day when the persecutor will come knocking at your door.
Adopt a compassionate and empathetic attitude, being ready to help, because mercy means truly feeling the pain and joy of another, thus forming a profound bond between you.

———————• •———————

4. False Persecution

It is important to make a distinction. There are people who feel persecuted even when there is no real threat. This phenomenon, known in psychology as "persecution mania" or "victim complex," reflects a distortion of perception. Those who fall into this trap see criticism as personal attacks and end up victimising themselves. Instead of accepting reality, they seek the attention of others by feigning suffering. It is essential to conduct an honest self-analysis to determine if the real problem lies within us.

Joseph Goebbels, the Nazi propaganda minister, once said that a lie that is repeated often enough becomes truth in people's minds. This manipulation technique is not limited to politics; it also applies on a personal level. If we keep telling ourselves we are persecuted, we risk believing this lie, even if it is not true. Therefore, we must be aware of this danger and avoid falling into the trap of our own imagination[110]. When you feel that everyone has something against you, the first step is to analyse yourself honestly. Perhaps the problem is not with others, but with you. It may be that no one is actually criticising you, but that you have fallen into a negative spiral and are martyring yourself.

Those who truly love God do not respond to challenges with bitterness or criticism, but with gentleness and kindness. Persecution should not be an excuse for negative behaviour; on the contrary, it is an opportunity to reflect God's love. True persecution comes from living out one's faith, not from

---

[110] Longerich, Peter. *Goebbels: A Biography*. Random House, 2015.

provocative or wrong actions that could have been avoided. If you are going through persecution, check whether it results from an authentic life with Christ and not from self-victimisation or a consequence of sin in your life.

People often think they are experiencing persecution when things do not go well for them—perhaps they feel persecuted by the government or maybe they lost their business or home. However, careful analysis may reveal that these difficulties are actually the consequences of their own mistakes or sinful actions.

For example, some choose not to pay their taxes, misinterpreting the biblical call to be *"wise as serpents" (Matthew 10:16, NKJV)*, and thinking they can find shortcuts. When the consequences of these choices arise, they consider themselves persecuted or tested in their faith, ignoring the fact that true persecution comes from living an authentic faith, not from breaking the law.

Of course, our Lord Jesus calls us to be *"wise as serpents and harmless as doves" (Matthew 10:16, NKJV)*, but this biblical wisdom does not mean seeking shortcuts or justifying wrongful behaviour; it means living with integrity and morality.

When things are not going well in our lives, we should ask ourselves if what we are experiencing is a form of genuine persecution for our sanctification or, rather, the consequences of wrong choices. If we deceive the state or lie, we cannot expect to be blessed. We may have more money temporarily, but we will suffer in other areas—physically, mentally, or even relationship-wise, and those around us will see us as a stumbling block.

———————• •———————

The devil never has good intentions for us and suffering that derives from wrongdoing is not a test of faith.

———————• •———————

It is important to remember that no one who has built their wealth on corruption has found true happiness. History is full of examples of people who, after accumulating riches through dishonest means, ended up suffering severe depression and even taking their own lives. Wealth gained through wrongful ways does not bring comfort, but becomes an increasingly heavy burden.[111]

Instead of finding excuses for our sins, we should ensure that we live as true servants of Christ, not of wrongdoing. Perhaps, at times, integrity will cost us financially, but God will take care of our needs. Jesus Christ Himself respected civil authorities and paid the necessary taxes (Matthew 17:24-27, NKJV). God will provide the resources we need to live honourably, and at the right time, He will reward us for our faithfulness.

"You are the light of the world," said the Saviour. *"A city that is set on a hill cannot be hidden" (Matthew 5:14, NKJV).* When we sin, it becomes visible to all those around us. Likewise,

---

[111] Schafer, John R. "The Psychopathology of Corruption." *Psychology Today*, August 2, 2018.

our good deeds are also visible. We are called to be examples of righteousness and light to others. A light is not put under a basket but on a lampstand, to give light to all (Matthew 5:15-16, NKJV).

Our deeds must be seen not to glorify ourselves, but to bring glory to God.

How have we come, then, to falsify faith and to find all sorts of spiritual justifications for the punishments received as a result of our wrongdoing? The tragedy of this type of Christianity occurs when people invent excuses to justify their blatant sins, instead of looking honestly into their lives and acknowledging their mistakes. We must not forget that we are called to live in the light, to be honest, and to give up any form of twisting divine teachings to excuse wrongful behaviour.

Do you wonder why so many people's mentalities among us have deteriorated? Perhaps it is time to look deep into our lives and ask ourselves: are we suffering because of the righteousness we live in Christ or because of the sin we have sunk into?

When you face genuine persecution, do not be discouraged! Persevere and declare with faith: *"I can do all things through Christ who strengthens me" (Philippians 4:13, NKJV).* The Holy Spirit has given you the power to endure any trial, for no temptation is greater than the power of God within you.

However, this power comes from your relationship with Christ, not from your own strategies, schemes, or worldly tactics. Many believers boast of their high positions, but true greatness comes only when God is the source of your worth. If you have gained progress through compromises, those victories are merely temporary and will not bring you eternal blessing. God cannot be deceived: *"For he who sows to his flesh will of the flesh reap corruption, but he who sows to the Spirit will of the Spirit reap everlasting life" (Galatians 6:7-8, NKJV).*

Be a light for those around you. Your good deeds will shine and draw people to God. However, if there is corruption and injustice in your life, how can others see you as an example of faith? Imagine that, on judgement day, you will stand face-to-face with those you have wronged. Your actions matter—they either speak of your true faith, or they will condemn you.

Though painful, persecution is sometimes necessary to purify us, helping us evaluate our actions and align ourselves correctly—with the side of good, not evil. It helps us separate the wheat from the chaff in our lives, allowing us to remain faithful to our Christian calling.

Do not be surprised by the trials you go through, but rejoice that you partake in the sufferings of Christ, so that when His glory is revealed, you may rejoice even more. *"If you are reproached for the name of Christ, blessed are you!" (1 Peter 4:12-14, NKJV).* But you cannot live in the Spirit of God if you continue to remain in sin. Be obedient to Christ, not merely a conformist. Those who truly listen to God place their entire trust in Him.

The Lord Jesus demonstrated what true obedience means by fulfilling the Father's will without hesitation. We too are called to live in the same way, trusting in God even when we are persecuted. Rejoice and be glad, even if you suffer for His Name. Bless those who persecute you, support them, and show them God's love. Just as God loved us, you are called to do the same. Persevere in your race, heed Christ, and live according to His commandments. Do everything He asks of you at the right time, and you will receive the promised blessings.

Chapter 18

The Traps Along the Path
to Happiness

Modern society has shaped our minds in such a way that we find ourselves endlessly chasing after happiness but rarely experiencing it fully. Why does it always seem to slip through our fingers? Because we've been conditioned to fall into subtle traps that divert us from the path to true happiness. These traps infiltrate our everyday lives through the norms and values imposed by the modern world. It's essential that we become aware of them and learn to avoid them when they arise.

Together, we'll examine twelve of these traps, so we can recognise and avoid them when we encounter them. Each trap hides an illusion, and understanding these illusions will help us walk wisely along the path to genuine, lasting happiness.

1. Negative Company

Atunci când te afli în preajma oamenilor negativi, viața ta vaWhen you surround yourself with negative people, your life will inevitably be influenced by pessimism and negative thoughts, which prevents you from finding happiness. Scientific studies confirm that the company we keep plays a crucial role in our emotional health. The phenomenon called "emotional contagion" describes our tendency to absorb others' emotions. This means that the emotional state of those around you can have a direct impact on your happiness and wellbeing. If you are surrounded by people who focus only on problems and never on solutions, you will start to internalise the same pattern of thinking.[112]

Positive psychology research emphasises the importance of healthy social relationships. Studies show that positive relationships contribute to wellbeing and surrounding yourself with optimistic and empathetic people can even improve your physical and mental health. In contrast, negative people can be sources of stress and anxiety, affecting our inner balance.[113]

The Bible warns us of this danger: *"Blessed is the man who walks not in the counsel of the ungodly" (Psalm 1:1, NKJV)*. This verse encourages us to evaluate our company and ensure we surround ourselves with people who nourish us spiritually and emotionally. Quality social support is crucial for preventing depression and anxiety.

To protect our mental health, it is important to set boundaries against negativity. Turn pessimistic conversations into

---

[112] Christakis, Nicholas A., and James H. Fowler. *Connected: The Surprising Power of Our Social Networks and How They Shape Our Lives*. Little, Brown and Company, 2009.
[113] Seligman, Martin E.P. *Flourish: A Visionary New Understanding of Happiness and Well-being*. Atria Books, 2011.

productive dialogues by asking those who complain how they plan to solve their problems.

Choosing the right company isn't just about personal preference; it's a decision that can profoundly impact your life. Science tells us that the people we surround ourselves with significantly shape our perception of reality and even our sense of identity.

———• •———

Surround yourself with people who inspire you and motivate you to become a better person, who bring optimism and encouragement into your life. Positive relationships can help you see the world more clearly and with greater hope. On the other hand, toxic relationships can drag you down, reducing your ability to see life with optimism and clarity.

———• •———

Anyone who makes you feel worthless or who creates anxiety in your life wastes your time and fills your life with grey clouds instead of helping you see the clear blue sky above.

2. Comparing Real Life to the Idealised Image on Social Media

Recent studies confirm that excessive use of social media is associated with an increased risk of envy and a decrease in life satisfaction. Leon Festinger's "social comparison theory" explains that people naturally tend to compare themselves to others to evaluate their own worth. On social media, this tendency is amplified because people only present the best aspects of their lives, creating a distorted image of reality.

Social media has significantly changed how we perceive our lives and relate to others. Filters and retouching create a distorted reality, leading users to fall into a dangerous trap, as comparing themselves to this manufactured reality can lead to frustration, anxiety, and even depression.

A study conducted by the Happiness Research Institute, known as the "Facebook Experiment," demonstrated the negative impact of social media on users' wellbeing. Participants who gave up Facebook for a week reported greater satisfaction with their lives and experienced less stress, anxiety, and loneliness than those who continued using the platform.[114] It's essential to look at our lives realistically and to avoid the trap of comparing ourselves to a fabricated reality.

People who post on social media only present their best moments, hiding their true struggles and imperfections. Instead of comparing ourselves to these illusory images, it's far healthier to focus on the genuine relationships and experiences in our own lives.

From a spiritual perspective, comparisons with others can be a dangerous trap that takes us away from our true purpose— to fulfil our unique calling before God. Scripture encourages us

---

[114] Meik Wiking, "The Little Book of Lykke: Secrets of the World's Happiest People," Happiness Research Institute, 2017.

to *"set your mind on things above, not on things on the earth"* *(Colossians 3:2, NKJV)*. When we focus too much on the lives of others and give in to envy towards their apparent successes, we risk losing sight of our own relationship with God.

Instead of seeking validation in the eyes of the world, we should seek fulfilment and happiness in our communion with God and the unique mission He has entrusted to us.

True happiness comes from living according to His will and serving Him with a sincere, devoted, and grateful heart.

3. Immunity to Wonder – Apathy

Indifference toward the world around us is a subtle but dangerous trap that keeps us from achieving true happiness. Apathy is defined as a lack of interest or emotion toward events that could be considered amazing or remarkable. When we lose our ability to be amazed by the little things in life, we gradually disconnect from the beauty of creation and the simple joys that give meaning to our existence.

Wonder is more than an emotion; it is a way of anchoring ourselves in the present, a means of appreciating the blessings of the day. Defined psychologically as an intense emotional state triggered by something new, surprising or grand, wonder brings about a "mental expansion" that opens the door to new perspectives and enriches our life experiences. Psychologist

Dacher Keltner, a pioneer in the study of awe, emphasises that this emotion not only improves our psychological state, but also increases empathy and generosity.[115]

However, in a world dominated by technology and constant stimuli, we gradually lose our ability to be impressed by what surrounds us. The world becomes more accessible and smaller, yet paradoxically less wondrous. This loss of wonder affects both our mental health and our relationships with others.

Research in social psychology shows that experiences that surprise and amaze us help lift us out of daily routines, allowing us to live more deeply. Wonder is associated with gratitude, wellbeing, and even a deep sense of belonging to something greater than ourselves. Without wonder, life becomes monotonous and lacks satisfaction. Indifference toward life's beauty robs us of the small joys that connect us to life and to each other.

From a spiritual perspective, wonder is a way of appreciating divine creation. Psalm 8:3-4 encourages us to look at the heavens and marvel at God's handiwork. This wonder draws us closer to the Creator and teaches us to live in gratitude and humility. *"Open my eyes, that I may see wondrous things from Your law" (Psalm 119:18, NKJV)* is an invitation to live with our eyes open to the beauty of creation and to see God's greatness in the small things of life.

---

[115] Keltner, Dacher. *Awe: The New Science of Everyday Wonder and How It Can Transform Your Life*. Penguin Press, 2023.

Regaining the ability to be surprised by simple things will bring us closer to true happiness. As the Psalmist urges us to keep our minds open to God's wonders, we too should open our eyes to the little moments of wonder in our daily lives.

4. Social Isolation and Lack of Fellowship

Social isolation, which stands in direct contrast to wonder and connecting with others, is a dangerous trap for those who, due to their profound apathy, choose to completely withdraw from interactions with others.

Isolation may seem like a solution to unhappiness, but in reality, it is a vicious cycle that only amplifies emotional discomfort.

Psychologists confirm that social isolation is one of the most damaging behaviours for both mental and physical health.[116]

Human beings are inherently social creatures, who were created to live and interact within a community. When God created us, He intended for us to enjoy fellowship and relationships with one another. Completely isolating ourselves due to unhappiness or personal problems is a major mistake. Though

---

[116] John T. Cacioppo and William Patrick, *Loneliness: Human Nature and the Need for Social Connection* (W.W. Norton & Company, 2008).

avoiding people might seem easier, this isolation only inten-sifies negative feelings. Every social interaction and conver-sation, even those that seem uncomfortable at first, can bring unexpected benefits. A word spoken at the right moment or just someone's presence can have a profound impact on your wellbeing.

Continual isolation becomes dangerous when it turns into a habit. Prolonged loneliness has a negative impact on the spir-it, mind, and even on faith. Therefore, it is crucial to recognise this trap and strive to avoid it.

A well-known study has shown that loneliness and social isolation are major risk factors for mortality, having an effect comparable to smoking 15 cigarettes a day. The study high-lights that the physical and psychological risks of loneliness are extremely serious and should be treated with the same concern as other recognised harmful behaviours.[117]

Even when unhappiness pushes us to withdraw, it is im-portant to remain open to others. Active participation in com-munity life can provide us with the emotional resources need-ed to overcome difficult moments.

Psalm 111:1 (NKJV) reminds us that *"in the assembly of the upright and in the congregation"* we find joy and the op-portunity to praise God.

---

[117] Holt-Lunstad, J., Smith, T. B., & Layton, J. B. (2015). Loneliness and social isolation as risk factors for mortality: A meta-analytic review. *American Psychologist, 70*(4), pp. 310–327. https://doi.org/10.1037/a0039736.

Fellowship with other believers is vital for our spiritual and mental health. God created us for relationships and community.

The apostle Paul emphasises the importance of the body of Christ, in which each member plays an essential role (1 Corinthians 12:12-27, NKJV). To remain isolated is to forfeit the gifts and blessings that God offers us through others, which has devastating effects on our physical and mental wellbeing.

5. Guilt

Guilt can become a major obstacle to happiness, especially when it is persistent and uncontrolled. When you feel guilty for everything happening around you, this emotion can overwhelm, terrorise, and wear you down. Guilt thus becomes a psychological mechanism that disrupts your inner peace and affects your relationships with others and even with yourself.

In psychology, guilt is considered a self-reproaching emotion that arises when a person feels they have violated moral or ethical standards. In moderate doses, guilt can be a positive force, prompting us to correct wrong behaviour and improve our relationships. However, chronic, prolonged guilt becomes harmful, triggering ongoing stress, anxiety, and even depression.[118]

---

[118] Peter R. Breggin, *Guilt, Shame, and Anxiety: Understanding and Overcoming Negative Emotions* (Prometheus Books, 2014).

———————• •———————

To overcome guilt,
the first step is identifying
the problem and taking
responsibility for it.

———————• •———————

Every problem has a solution, and regaining control over your life requires a conscious effort to resolve the situation. It is essential to break out of denial and address guilt actively— seek forgiveness, resolve conflicts, and in doing so, happiness will begin to return to your life. However, forgiveness doesn't come just from resolving our problems with others, but from genuine personal reconciliation with God. This reconciliation restores emotional and spiritual balance, and guilt no longer has power over us.

"Create in me a clean heart, O God, and renew a stead- fast spirit within me" (Psalm 51:10, NKJV). Joy and happiness come from the assurance of salvation, and this assurance is achieved through confession of sins and reconciliation with God. *"If we confess our sins, He is faithful and just to forgive us" (1 John 1:9, NKJV).*

As long as you allow yourself to be overwhelmed by guilt and to remain isolated, happiness will remain inaccessible. Only by taking responsibility, reconciling with God, and making an effort to correct mistakes will you regain inner peace.

6. Perfectionism and Excessive Self-Control

Perfectionism and excessive self-control are major obstacles to happiness because they prevent you from accepting any outcome that doesn't meet an imposed standard. Perfection is often an impossible ideal, and exaggerated ambitions become sources of frustration. When you try to control every aspect of your life, you end up unhappy, irritating those around you, and living under constant self-imposed pressure.

Healthy self-control is essential for maintaining discipline and balance in life. However, when it becomes excessive, self-control turns into a burden. Perfectionism and the desire for absolute control are often linked to anxiety, as any deviation from imposed standards causes unease and a deep sense of failure.

A common example is parents who try to control every detail of their children's lives. These children grow up in a strict environment, lacking freedom and creativity. Instead of being encouraged to explore their talents and learn from mistakes, they end up living according to their parents' desires and fears. Thus, these children do not develop fully and are unable to discover their true potential.

It is essential to recognise that perfectionism not only prevents us from being happy, but also affects our relationships with others. Trying to control everyone around us reveals a lack of trust in their abilities, as well as inner insecurity.

Finding a balance between self-control and flexibility, between striving for excellence and accepting imperfection, is the key to a balanced and happy life.

God calls us to trust in Him, not to try to control everything. Trusting in the divine plan helps us overcome this trap of excessive control. As Scripture tells us: *"Trust in the Lord with all your heart, and lean not on your own understanding" (Proverbs 3:5, NKJV)*. By letting God guide our steps, we can find true peace and freedom from the need to control everything.

7. Chronic Dissatisfaction

Momentary dissatisfaction and chronic dissatisfaction are two distinct manifestations of negativity. Generally, dissatisfaction is a negative reaction to what we are offered, to our achievements, or to how others behave. On the other hand, chronic dissatisfaction involves an inability to recognise and appreciate the efforts of those around us, be they small gestures or personal sacrifices.[119]

By constantly complaining and continuously criticising others, a chronically dissatisfied person reinforces their own negativity.

---

[119] Campbell, Debra. *Understanding Your Chronic Dissatisfaction: A Guide to Emotional Freedom and Self-Compassion*. CreateSpace Independent Publishing Platform, 2017.

Over time, chronic dissatisfaction becomes a trap that perpetuates unhappiness, generating stress and inner conflicts.

When you repeatedly focus on the negative aspects of life, they become the centre of your existence.

By contrast, Scripture urges us to show gratitude in all things. Ephesians 5:20 (NKJV) teaches us to give thanks to God regardless of circumstances because true blessings are sometimes hidden under the guise of difficulties. A grateful mindset brings peace and happiness, while constant dissatisfaction perpetuates frustration and makes the path to a meaningful life more difficult.

Often encountered in modern society, chronic dissatisfaction distances us from genuine happiness. We are often tempted to constantly seek more without appreciating what we already have. While the desire to improve is natural, it is essential to not develop a spirit of permanent dissatisfaction. Happiness comes from balancing the desire for better with gratitude for the blessings we have already received.

8. The Need for External Validation

The trap of wanting to impress others lies in the tendency to seek external validation, to earn the admiration of others.

This is a dangerous mentality because happiness becomes dependent on the reactions of others, making it unstable and fragile. When you focus too much on the impression you make on those around you, you lose authenticity, and this behaviour can lead to unhappiness. Not everyone will be impressed, and this reality can lead to disappointment and frustration.

Psychologists emphasise that this need to impress is often linked to deep insecurity. Carl Rogers, one of the founders of humanistic psychology, stresses the importance of authentic behaviour and unconditional acceptance for a balanced life. When we focus on external impressions, we risk losing touch with our true selves. Instead of relying on others' validation, we should focus on building a healthy confidence in our own values and abilities.[120]

When we excessively focus on the impression we make on others, not only do we waste emotional energy, but we also underestimate our own values and abilities. This behaviour exposes us to the trap of constantly comparing ourselves to others, creating an endless cycle of insecurity and dissatisfaction. Instead of relying on external validation, we should turn our attention to developing genuine confidence in our own qualities and talents.

Another aspect of this trap is the tendency to evaluate our personal worth based on visible success. This approach can

[120] Rogers, Carl R. *On Becoming a Person: A Therapist's View of Psychotherapy.* Houghton Mifflin Harcourt, 1995.

create constant pressure, leading to emotional exhaustion and even depression when our attempts to impress fail.

———• •———

It is essential to develop a set of solid, biblically based internal values that do not depend on others' approval. This will offer us true happiness that springs from within rather than from the accolades of others.

———• •———

On a spiritual level, this trap is related to pride and vanity, both of which are criticised in numerous religious traditions. In Christianity, Scripture teaches us to focus on humility and on good deeds done with a pure purpose and not to impress others. *"And whatever you do, do it heartily, as to the Lord and not to men" (Colossians 3:23, NKJV).* Thus, the purpose of our actions should not be the admiration of others, but sincere dedication to spiritual principles and values.

9. Negativity

The trap of negativity is one of the most subtle yet dangerous barriers to happiness. Life doesn't always turn out the way we want, and inevitably, we will encounter obstacles and difficult situations. However, when we focus solely on the negative aspects, we amplify our unhappiness. Negativity becomes a mental habit that prevents us from seeing the good around us and being grateful for the positive things in life.

Happy people are not those who have no problems, but those who take the time to find positive things, even in the midst of difficulties.

Instead of complaining about what's not going well, they choose to reflect on what is working and what they are grateful for. Psychology teaches us that this process of reframing reality, known as cognitive restructuring, helps us change our perspective and focus on the positive aspects. Research shows that an optimistic outlook reduces stress levels and improves mental health.

Negativity can become a "self-fulfilling prophecy." When you focus only on what might go wrong, there's a high probability that those very things will happen because your mind is already set on failure, and you end up sabotaging yourself. To avoid the trap of negativity, it is essential to practice active optimism. Identifying things you are grateful for each day can improve your overall state and help you see opportunities where you once saw only problems.

A spiritual example can be found in the Bible, where the apostle Paul urges us: *"Rejoice in the Lord always. Again I will say, rejoice!" (Philippians 4:4, NKJV).* This call to joy doesn't ignore life's problems but invites us to find reasons for gratitude and trust in God, even in the midst of difficulties. By choosing a mindset of gratitude and joy, we can free ourselves from the trap of negativity and come closer to genuine happiness.

10. Neglecting Goals

Neglecting goals creates chaos in our lives, bringing confusion and a lack of direction. When we don't have clear markers and well-defined goals, we feel lost and unhappy. Without a concrete target, our efforts seem to lead nowhere, fuelling frustration and disappointment.

In Philippians 3:12-14 (NKJV), the Apostle Paul emphasises the importance of having a clear purpose in life. He speaks of running towards a well-defined goal which motivates him to keep going regardless of the challenges he faces. Even in prison, Paul maintained his hope and focus, anchoring himself in a higher spiritual perspective.

From a psychological standpoint, setting goals is essential for living a balanced and happy life. Studies show that people who set clear and measurable goals live more fulfilled lives and experience less stress. These objectives give us direction and motivate us to persevere, even in the face of challenges.[121]

A chaotic lifestyle without clear markers creates a constant sense of disorientation. Conversely, by organising our lives around well-defined goals, we can enjoy the journey more and adapt more easily to changes, increasing our chances of experiencing true happiness.

---

[121] Locke, E.A., & Latham, G.P. (2002). *Building a Practically Useful Theory of Goal Setting and Task Motivation: A 35-Year Odyssey.*

11. Fear

Fear is an omnipresent emotion born out of the perception of real or imagined dangers. This natural response can be amplified or diminished by our thoughts and perceptions. Facing our fears is essential to reducing their influence over our lives. The process of "desensitisation" helps us confront fear in a controlled manner, removing its power to paralyse us and sabotage our happiness.

Another critical aspect is the social context. The people around us have a significant impact on how we manage fear. A positive and supportive circle that helps you face life's challenges by offering understanding, encouragement, and assistance can reduce anxiety and fear, giving us the courage to overcome challenges. As Psalm 23:4 (NKJV) reminds us: *"Yea, though I walk through the valley of the shadow of death, I will fear no evil; for You are with me"*. The presence of God, along with the support of loved ones, can help us conquer our fears and transform these emotions into a constructive element rather than an obstacle.

12. Ignoring the Present for the Past or the Future

This trap is particularly insidious, as it robs us of the ability to live in the present. Some people remain captive to the past, constantly reminiscing about the "good old days." At the same time, others either build their lives on dreams of a perfect future, entirely ignoring the present, or are paralysed by fears and scenarios that haven't happened yet. Both attitudes create a vicious cycle where today's reality is neglected, and happiness becomes inaccessible.

Living in the past can serve as a defence mechanism against present disappointments, but ultimately it becomes an anchor that ties us to regrets and mistakes. Psychologists warn that such excessive focus on the past can lead to depression, anxiety, and a sense of meaninglessness.

Similarly, living exclusively in the future without paying attention to the present turns us into dreamers without action or people paralysed by fear. This mindset allows us to avoid today's responsibilities, hoping that the future will bring all the answers. In reality, this type of thinking prevents us from taking the necessary steps to build the future we desire.

The correct approach is to stay anchored in the present, learn from the past, and plan for the future.

Psychologically, this balance helps us be aware of the moment's reality, act proactively, and use past lessons to guide our decisions. It is also important to accept the uncertainty of the future. As Proverbs 19:21 (NKJV) teaches: *"There are many plans in a man's heart, nevertheless the Lord's counsel—that will stand".*

From a spiritual perspective, the Bible urges us to focus on today, living in the present moment with gratitude and trust in God. In Matthew 6:34 (NKJV), we are told: *"Therefore do not worry about tomorrow, for tomorrow will worry about*

313

its own things. Sufficient for the day is its own trouble". This spiritual wisdom encourages us to live in the present, using lessons from the past and having faith that God will guide our steps in the future.

Throughout our life, we often encounter obstacles that can steal our happiness and divert us from our true purpose. The traps we've explored—whether it's the temptation to impress others, the trap of neglecting goals, or the paralysing power of fear—are challenges that test our resilience and wisdom. The key to overcoming these barriers lies in living intentionally, staying anchored in the present, learning from past lessons, and planning for the future with faith and trust in God. True happiness is not something external; it is a state of mind that comes from aligning our thinking with spiritual truths and embracing the life that God has given us.

As we draw near to the conclusion of this journey toward happiness, it is essential to recognise that happiness also comes from understanding and learning from the mistakes of those who struggle with unhappiness. In this final section, we will explore the stories of unhappy people and the valuable lessons their mistakes offer us about recovery and getting back on the right path. Through their experiences, we gain insights into avoiding these traps and, with the help of divine grace, we will be able to return to the path of fulfilment and joy.

Chapter 19

———— ❦ ————

Unhappy People – Lessons on Mistakes and Recovery

Throughout this book, we explored various aspects of spiritual and mental life that can either bring us closer to or distance us from true happiness. We discussed the importance of cultivating the right mindset, genuine faith, the challenges of persecution, and the role of wisdom in everyday life. We learned that happiness does not come merely from external circumstances, but from a profound transformation of our thinking and character, in alignment with divine principles. Therefore, it is crucial to also speak about unhappy people— those who, despite their desire to be happy, remain trapped in the pitfalls of a misguided mindset and a life lacking spiritual direction. These people can teach us valuable lessons about what it truly means to live in harmony with God's will.

Unhappiness is not always the result of a life filled with external failures. It often stems from how we choose to perceive and respond to life circumstances. An unhappy person may appear to have everything they want in the eyes of the world: success, money, and relationships; yet, inside, they live with an emptiness that material things cannot fill. It is a void that appears when one loses their connection with God, when their values become confused, and when they build their life on unstable foundations.

Despite their apparent prosperity, these people are often stuck in self-destructive mindsets. They constantly compare their lives with those of others, place their happiness in the hands of others' approval, and sabotage their own wellbeing through negative thinking. This unhappiness arises from superficial desires and the need for external validation, and as they pursue these goals, they become increasingly alienated from their true spiritual calling.

Wisdom teaches us that happiness is not an end in itself, but a result of living an ethical and moral life—a life based on truth, love, and compassion for others.

Unhappy people are often trapped in a spiral of unfulfillment precisely because they focus their energy on the wrong goals. They seek to accumulate material goods, gain power, or build an image of success, but without a spiritual foundation, all of this proves insufficient.

This state of unhappiness serves as a warning to those who are about to fall into the same traps. It is an alarm that urges us to reconsider our priorities and realign our thinking with eternal values that bring true happiness. The Bible repeatedly warns us about this danger: *"For what will it profit a man if he gains the whole world, and loses his own soul?" (Mark 8:36, NKJV)*. This rhetorical question reminds us that no matter how much we accumulate in this world, it will all be in vain if we neglect our spiritual health.

———• •———

So, what do unhappy people teach us?
They show us that authentic happiness
cannot be found in the fleeting things
of this world, but only in our relationship
with God.

———• •———

They are a living testimony that without a solid spiritual foundation, life becomes a pursuit of the wind—meaningless and unfulfilled. Let us learn from their mistakes and seek true happiness in the things that truly matter: faith, love, and obedience to God.

It is time to change our mindset, recalibrate our lives, and place our hope in eternal things, not in the ephemeral. In the end, true happiness is reserved for those who put their trust in God and, through wisdom, choose to build their life on a solid and eternal foundation.

So, how can we become people with a healthy mindset who do not fall into traps that lead us away from happiness?

As we have learned, living a happy and fulfilled life requires being aware of how our own thinking can become a major obstacle. A misguided mindset, formed from superficial desires, constant comparisons, and the need for external validation, is one of the main sources of unhappiness. We often sabotage our own happiness through attitudes and habits that block our access to genuine joy. Understanding this reality is a crucial step toward profound and lasting change, for true happiness comes from transforming our mindset and aligning our thinking with the correct principles and values that bring fulfilment.

An old English proverb offers us a valuable lesson: "Bees don't waste their time explaining to flies that honey is better than manure." Bees are happy only if they live in their beneficial environment. Likewise, to find the path to complete happiness, we must carefully examine everything that motivates us in this life—the honey of divine mindset or the manure of the world.

The foundation of our character is built on faith, a faith that develops through learning and personal discovery. Faith is not inherited; it springs from our relationship with God and our life experiences. In this sense, it is important to remember that our values and beliefs can be nourished from two sources: one divine, based on ethics and morality, and the other corrupt, born of immediate and selfish human desires. To discern between these sources, each of us must wisely examine our own life. However, wisdom is not easily attained—it requires will, motivation, and a sustained effort to be learned, applied, and embedded in our minds.

In the previous chapters, we discussed the exhortation to be "wise as serpents" (Matthew 10:16). What does this mean, or more simply, how can we consider serpents wise?

Referring to Genesis 3:1 (NKJV), we find that the serpent was *"more cunning than any beast of the field."* The term "nahash" in biblical Hebrew is usually translated as "serpent," but some scholars suggest that this word could have other connotations, such as "the shining one" or "the imposing one," indicating a being with a much higher status. This interpretation reflects the idea that Satan used words and wisdom to distort the truth and tempt humanity.[122]

Satan manipulated the power of words, distorting their meaning to overturn the glory that humanity received from God. This text highlights the power found in the skilful use of words. As humans, we are called to use information, knowledge, and wisdom in a biblical, undistorted way—to uplift, not to destroy. This is God's calling in the verse, "Be wise as serpents…" (Matthew 10:16): to use wisdom and knowledge to build and correct.

An often-misunderstood aspect is that our minds can control our lives if not educated correctly. Therefore, it is crucial to educate our children from an early age, filling their minds with information that will later become sources of life. As Scripture

---

[122] Michael S. Heiser, *The Unseen Realm: Recovering the Supernatural Worldview of the Bible* (Bellingham, WA: Lexham Press, 2015).

says: "Out of the abundance of the heart [of one's mind] the mouth speaks" (Matthew 12:34, NKJV). Wisdom helps us use these resources in the right way, to build a blessed and meaningful life.[123]

Human reasoning is a superior faculty that allows us to reflect on reality and respond to life's challenges. Its functioning can be influenced either by intelligence or by wisdom. Although we are all endowed with intelligence, it is not sufficient to guide us through life. Intelligence can be compared to the bricks that make up the structure of our thinking, but wisdom represents the way these bricks are arranged. Wisdom can either build a solid edifice of happiness or a fortress that isolates us in unhappiness. While intelligence is a divine gift, wisdom is earned through experience and continuous reflection.

If we wish to avoid the pitfalls of life and find true happiness, we must listen to, accept, and apply divine teaching, cultivating an authentic ethical and moral mindset. Ultimately, as it is written: *"The fear of the Lord is the beginning of wisdom"* (*Psalm 111:10, NKJV*). This fear should not be understood as a constraining dread, but rather as a profound and reverent respect.

———————————— • • ————————————

***We cannot truly love someone
without respecting them, and profound***

---

[123] Carol S. Dweck, *Mindset: The New Psychology of Success* (New York: Ballantine Books, 2007).

respect for God is the foundation of a life filled with wisdom.

————————• •———————

We live in a complex society that challenges us on multiple levels—spiritual, relational, both in our relationship with others and with ourselves. It is a society that often treats spiritual matters as mere linguistic clichés, distancing us from true happiness and fulfilment, no matter how much we try to follow the world's superficial prescriptions.

In this context, we often make two fundamental mistakes:

The first mistake is that we over-spiritualise matters and ignore the importance of wisdom. We believe that merely using spiritual concepts mechanically will lead us to the maturity needed to live wisely. But building something lasting requires conscious effort, motivation, and the expenditure of energy.

Some of us come to the mistaken conclusion that it is not essential to understand, but to just believe. This is an error, because authentic faith is born out of a deep understanding of reality, a recognition of the need for change, and the adoption of a correct mindset. *"So then faith comes by hearing, and hearing by the word of God" (Romans 10:17, NKJV).* In other words, we must hear and understand the Word in order to have genuine faith. If someone asks us to believe without investigation, we must be cautious, for even God exhorts us to *"test all things; hold fast what is good" (1 Thessalonians 5:21, NKJV).*

The second mistake is relying exclusively on worldly wisdom – which is transient – without seeking divine wisdom. Although some may overcome the effects of the first mistake, they may end up using the power of words to destroy instead of building. One of the greatest dangers is the tendency to relax our spiritual vigilance, accepting ideas and practices that lack a biblical or spiritual foundation. In the name of grace and love, we adopt erroneous rituals and philosophies without investing our energy in understanding and analysing them correctly. In doing so, we expose ourselves to immense spiritual risk and lose sight of our life's true purpose.

Scripture urges us: *"Gird up the loins of your mind, be sober, and rest your hope fully upon the grace that is to be brought to you at the revelation of Jesus Christ"* (1 Peter 1:13, NKJV). This imagery of "girding up the loins" evokes preparation for a task of great importance. Just as a woman gathers her strength to give birth, we too must invest effort and dedication to build a life based on truth and righteousness.

"Keep your heart with all diligence, for out of it spring the issues of life. Put away from you a deceitful mouth, and put perverse lips far from you" (Proverbs 4:23-24, NKJV). To distinguish between truth and falsehood, it is essential to investigate, understand, and adjust our course in the wisest possible way. *"Let your eyes look straight ahead, and your eyelids look right before you. Ponder the path of your feet, and let all your ways be established; do not turn to the right or the left; remove your foot from evil"* (Proverbs 4:25-27, NKJV).

If we want to change our mindset to lead our lives toward happiness, we must learn to let go of habits that do not help us in the process of personal transformation. It is our responsibility to become people who bring hope, joy, and grace.

Regardless of life's circumstances, the mindset we adopt determines whether we become the best or worst version of ourselves.

The only way to avoid extremes is to understand reality and use wisdom to change our lives for the better.

Today, many people struggle with a mindset that distances them from authentic happiness. Two fundamental needs often fuel this mindset:

1. The Need for Affluence:

Consumer society has implanted the idea that happiness is found in the accumulation of material resources, wealth, or financial goods, leading to a lifestyle oriented toward consumption and materialism. A person dominated by this need imagines they will be happy when they buy their first car or a valuable object. However, the joy brought by these things is short-lived, and the desire for more constantly reappears. This is one of the traps of modern society, making us chase after fleeting things and forgetting that true happiness does not come from accumulating material objects, but from a balanced life anchored in spiritual value.[124]

Studies have shown that although affluence can provide financial comfort, it is not directly proportional to long-term happiness. Psychologically, excessive affluence can even generate negative effects, such as increased anxiety and depression. A study published in the *Journal of Consumer Research* suggests that people tend to be happier when investing in experiences rather than material goods, as experiences contribute more to personal identity and the creation of lasting memories.[125]

2. The Need for Personal Peace—Different from the Peace of Christ:

Many of us desire to be left alone, to retreat into our comfort zones, away from life's responsibilities or problems. Isolation will not bring us happiness; on the contrary, it will cause us to lose connection with what truly matters.

Psychological studies show that humans are social beings, and isolation can have negative effects on both mental and physical health. For example, research conducted by Julianne Holt-Lunstad and colleagues has demonstrated that social isolation can increase the risk of premature mortality, comparable to other major health risks like obesity and smoking. Instead of

---

[124] Tim Kasser, *The High Price of Materialism*. MIT Press, 2002.

[125] Van Boven, Leaf, and Thomas Gilovich. "To Do or to Have? That Is the Question." *Journal of Consumer Research*, vol. 36, no. 1, 2009, pp. 14-27.

bringing happiness, withdrawal from society can amplify feelings of unhappiness and loneliness.[126]

Research also suggests that avoiding responsibilities and retreating into comfort zones can diminish the sense of personal fulfilment. This constant tendency to avoid can lead to a loss of control over one's life and an increase in feelings of helplessness, thereby reducing overall wellbeing and happiness.[127]

From a spiritual perspective, *"the peace of Christ"* is different from passive personal peace. The peace of Christ, as described in Scripture (*"Peace I leave with you, My peace I give to you; not as the world gives do I give to you"* - John 14:27, NKJV), is not merely the absence of conflict but an inner calm that transcends external circumstances, coming from trust and relationship with God.

Unlike personal peace, which relies on avoiding problems, the peace of Christ involves the courage to face life's challenges, trusting that God is with us.[128]

---

[126] Holt-Lunstad, Julianne, et al. "Loneliness and Social Isolation as Risk Factors for Mortality: A Meta-Analytic Review." *Perspectives on Psychological Science*, vol. 10, no. 2, 2015, pp. 227–237.

[127] Seligman, Martin E.P. "Learned Helplessness: A Theory for the Age of Personal Control." Oxford University Press, 1993.

[128] Foster, Richard J. *"Celebration of Discipline: The Path to Spiritual Growth."* HarperOne, 2018.

Instead of withdrawing from challenges, we should actively engage in life, connect with others, and seek authentic peace, which comes from managing responsibilities with wisdom and trust. Isolation and avoidance will not bring happiness, but only a temporary form of calm that ultimately can lead to unhappiness and disconnection.

To find the peace of Christ, it is essential to open our hearts to others, live in harmony with divine values, and cultivate genuine relationships. True peace does not come from avoiding problems, but from the ability to face them with faith and courage, knowing that God is our source of strength.

In the pursuit of authentic happiness, it is therefore crucial to evaluate our fundamental needs and ask ourselves if they are truly in alignment with God's plan for our lives. If we want to live a fulfilled and happy life, we must detach ourselves from the superficial mindset of the world, give up the obsessive pursuit of material affluence, and avoid the illusion of passive peace.

To understand the reasons behind this mindset in our society, it is essential to explore three key aspects: social comparison, peer pressure, and the compromise of values. These mechanisms profoundly influence our thinking and behaviour often leading us away from authentic happiness and moral values.

1. Social Comparison

Social comparison is the process by which we evaluate ourselves in relation to others, either to gain validation or to better define our position in the world. In modern society, influenced by social media and mass media, we are constantly bombarded with idealised images of success, beauty, and happiness. This dynamic conditions us to continuously compare ourselves to those around us, whether they are people we know in everyday life or celebrities and influencers online. Upward comparison—where we measure ourselves against those perceived to be better than us—can lead to anxiety, insecurity, and depression.

Psychologist Leon Festinger, through his Social Comparison Theory, emphasised that this tendency is natural, but that in the digital age, it can become destructive.

———• •———

Constant comparison distances us
from authentic happiness
because we seek external validation
instead of anchoring our value
in who we truly are.

———• •———

Scripture reminds us that *"the Lord does not see as man sees; for man looks at the outward appearance, but the Lord looks at the heart" (1 Samuel 16:7, NKJV)*. Instead of measuring ourselves by the world's standards, we should focus on what truly matters: our relationship with God and the integrity of our hearts.

2. Peer Pressure

Peer pressure is a powerful social force that affects not only teenagers, but adults as well. This pressure can influence our decisions and behaviours, causing us to conform to group norms to avoid social exclusion. Classic studies by psychologist Solomon Asch demonstrated just how powerful this impulse to conform can be, even when we know that the group's norms are wrong.[129]

From a spiritual perspective, peer pressure can become a significant test for those who wish to live according to moral principles and religious faith. The apostle Paul warns us: *"And do not be conformed to this world, but be transformed by the renewing of your mind" (Romans 12:2, NKJV).* In the face of peer pressure, integrity becomes an essential virtue. It takes courage to go against the current when our values are tested. Only by relying on divine wisdom can we maintain our spiritual identity intact and resist the temptations to compromise.

3. Lies and Compromise of Values

Lying and compromising values can severely erode self-esteem and psychological health. Social psychology shows that when we violate our own moral values, cognitive dissonance arises—a feeling of psychological discomfort that occurs when our behaviours contradict our beliefs[130]. This discomfort can lead us to try to justify our actions or even change our beliefs to reduce the inner tension.

---

[129] Zimbardo, P. (2007). *The Lucifer Effect: Understanding How Good People Turn Evil.* Random House.

[130] Festinger, L. (1957). *A Theory of Cognitive Dissonance.* Stanford University Press

However, compromising values harms us in the long run, affecting our integrity and inner wellbeing. In Scripture, the story of Ananias and Sapphira warns us of the dangers of lying and moral compromise. The true reward comes not from making compromises, but from upholding righteousness and moral principles, regardless of the temptations we encounter.

In conclusion, God offers us the opportunity to change our mindset and to become strong rocks amid life's storms. Authentic happiness is not found in constant comparisons with others, conforming to the world's norms, or compromising personal values. It comes from living a life of integrity, faith, and divine wisdom. In a world that often urges us to sell our souls for thirty pieces of silver, we are called to be steadfast rocks, to remain firm in faith, and not to yield to the pressures of modern society.

Through the lessons of the seven spiritual antechambers we have explored, we learned that true happiness comes from inner transformation, when we align our thinking with eternal values and refuse to compromise with what is evil. Each of us is called to be a light in the midst of darkness, to remain anchored in faith, and to show kindness, knowing that the true reward lies in God's Kingdom.

Regardless of life's circumstances, choosing to live a life centred on divine values protects us from the traps of the modern world and leads us to lasting and authentic happiness. In the end, each of us must make the conscious choice to remain faithful to our spiritual calling, even when it comes with challenges.

Conclusion

Our journey toward happiness, as we explored it together in this book, is not without its challenges. It is a complex path where each step involves self-discovery and the need to overcome the subtle obstacles that modern society presents. Ultimately, happiness is not a final destination, but a continuous choice—a way of living that is marked by gratitude, empathy, integrity, and faith.

Throughout this book, we explored each of the seven antechambers leading to happiness together, and we learned how to gain wisdom and mature our mindset. We discovered the importance of cultivating a life based on solid values and analysed the pitfalls that can lead us astray—from negative influences in our surroundings to the tendency to remain stuck in the past or excessively worry about the future.

Now, at the end of this journey, we can certainly say that true happiness does not come from external sources, material possessions, or social recognition. It stems from within—from authentic relationships, from our attitude toward life, and from how we choose to relate to others and to God. Happiness is a personal choice. It is the daily decision to focus on what truly matters, to free ourselves from the burdens of the past, and not to be paralysed by fears of the future.

Happy people are those who have learned to live each moment with joy, to overcome their fears, and to share their blessings with others. They have understood that absolute happiness is not an end in itself, but the natural result of a life lived in harmony with God's will. It is the natural conclusion of an existence guided by love, empathy, justice, and faith.

I hope that this journey has helped you discover new perspectives on life and provided you with a practical guide to becoming a happy person—one who brings joy to those around them. True happiness is a state of mind – one that is built daily through conscious choices, a life lived with meaning, integrity, and a deep connection with God.

Thank you for your trust; I wish you will find that inner peace that comes from a life filled with meaning and love. May the divine smile always be upon your lips and may His joy fill your heart day after day!

References

[1] Bauman, Z. (2000). *Liquid modernity*. Polity Press.

[2] Waldinger, R. J., & Schulz, M. S. (2016). The long reach of nurturing family environments: Links with midlife emotion-regulatory styles and late-life security in intimate relationships.

[3] Twenge, J. M., & Kasser, T. (2013). Generational changes in materialism and work centrality, 1976–2007: Associations with temporal changes in societal insecurity and materialistic role modeling. *Personality and Social Psychology Bulletin, 39*(7), pp. 883-897. https://doi.org/10.1177/0146167213484586

[4] Ajzen, I. (1991). The theory of planned behavior. *Organizational Behavior and Human Decision Processes, 50*(2), pp. 179-211.

[5] Haidt, J. (2012). *The righteous mind: Why good people are divided by politics and religion*. Vintage Books.

[6] Willard, D. (1998). *The divine conspiracy: Rediscovering our hidden life in God*. HarperOne.

[7] Dweck, C. S. (2006). *Mindset: The New Psychology of Success*. Random House Incorporated.

[8] Lewis, C. S. (2001). *Mere Christianity*. HarperOne.

[9] Warren, R. (2002). *The purpose driven life: What on earth am I here for?* Zondervan.

[10] Burgo, J. (2015). *The narcissist you know: Defending yourself against extreme narcissists in an all-about-me age.* Touchstone.

[11] Brown, B. (2012). *Daring greatly: How the courage to be vulnerable transforms the way we live, love, parent, and lead.* Avery.

[12] Brooks, D. (2015). *The road to character*. Random House.

[13] Banaji, M. R., & Greenwald, A. G. (2013). *Blindspot: Hidden biases of good people.* Delacorte Press.

[14] Amodio, D. M., & Cikara, M. (2021). The social neuroscience of prejudice. *Annual Review of Psychology, 72*, pp. 439-469. https://doi.org/10.1146/annurev-psych-010419-050928

[15] Towers, A., Williams, M. N., Hill, S. R., & Philipp, M. C. (2016). What makes for the most intense regrets? Comparing the effects of several theoretical predictors of regret intensity. *Frontiers in Psychology, 7*, Article 1941. https://doi.org/10.3389/fpsyg.2016.01941

[16] Roese, N. J. (2005). *If only: How to turn regret into opportunity*. Broadway Books.

[17] Landa, A., Fallon, B. A., Wang, Z., Duan, Y., Liu, F., Wager, T. D., Ochsner, K., & Peterson, B. S. (2020). When it hurts even more: The neural dynamics of pain and interpersonal emotions. *Journal of Psychosomatic Research, 128*, 109881. https://doi.org/10.1016/j.jpsychores.2019.109881

[18] Matarazzo, O., Abbamonte, L., Greco, C., Pizzini, B., & Nigro, G. (2021). Regret and other emotions related to decision-making: Antecedents, appraisals, and phenomenological aspects. *Frontiers in Psychology, 12*, Article 783248. https://doi.org/10.3389/fpsyg.2021.783248

[19] Roese, N. J. (2005). *If only: How to turn regret into opportunity*. Broadway Books.

[20] Strong, J. (1890). *Strong's Exhaustive Concordance of the Bible*. Public Domain.

[21] Woodley, R. (2012). *Shalom and the community of creation: An indigenous vision*. Eerdmans.

[22] Lewis, C. S. (2001). *Mere Christianity*. HarperOne.

[23] Magill, R. J. Jr. (2012). *Sincerity: How a moral ideal born five hundred years ago inspired religious wars, modern art, hipster chic, and the curious notion that we all have something to say (no matter how dull)*. W. W. Norton & Company.

[24] Ariely, D. (2012). *The honest truth about dishonesty: How we lie to everyone–especially ourselves*. HarperCollins.

25 Lee, K. (2013). Little Liars: Development of verbal deception in children. *Child Development Perspectives, 7*(2), pp. 91-96. https://doi.org/10.1111/cdep.12023

26 Feldman, R. S. (2006). Liar, Liar: Deception in everyday life. *American Scientist, 94*(6), pp. 515-517. https://www.jstor.org/stable/27858701

27 Tavris, C., & Aronson, E. (2015). *Mistakes were made (but not by me): Why we justify foolish beliefs, bad decisions, and hurtful acts.* Mariner Books.

28 Bok, S. (1999). *Lying: Moral choice in public and private life.* Vintage Books.

29 Gibbs, R. W. (1994). *The poetics of mind: Figurative thought, language, and understanding.* Cambridge University Press.

30 Tavris, C., & Aronson, E. (2015). *Mistakes were made (but not by me): Why we justify foolish beliefs, bad decisions, and hurtful acts.* Mariner Books.

31 DePaulo, B. M. (2016). The many faces of lies. În A. G. Miller (Ed.), *The social psychology of good and evil* (2nd ed., pp. 227–248). The Guilford Press.

32 Vrij, A. (2008). *Detecting lies and deceit: Pitfalls and opportunities.* Wiley.

33 Von Hippel, W., & Trivers, R. (2011). The evolution and psychology of self-deception. *Behavioral and Brain Sciences, 34*(1), pp. 1-56. https://doi.org/10.1017/S0140525X10001354

[34] Tversky, A., & Kahneman, D. (1981). The framing of decisions and the psychology of choice. *Science, 211*(4481), pp. 453-458. https://doi.org/10.1126/science.7455683

[35] Henry, M. (1961). *Matthew Henry's commentary on the whole Bible.* Zondervan Publishing House.

[36] Hokkaido University. June 21, 2018. How do horses read human emotional cues? *ScienceDaily.* https://www.sciencedaily.com/releases/2018/06/180621141926.htm

[37] *Oxford Handbook of Positive Psychology.* (2024). Humility and interpersonal relationships. Oxford Academic. https://academic.oup.com

[38] Magonet, J. (2024). *Numbers: An introduction and study guide: A new translation with introduction and commentary.* Oxford University Press.

[39] Foster, R. J. (2018). *Celebration of discipline: The path to spiritual growth.* HarperOne.

[40] Peterson, J. B. (2018). *12 rules for life: An antidote to chaos.* Random House Canada.

[41] Cialdini, R. B. (2006). *Influence: The psychology of persuasion.* Harper Business.

[42] Milgram, S. (2009). *Obedience to authority: An experimental view.* Harper Perennial.

[43] Cialdini, R. B. (2006). *Influence: The psychology of persuasion.* Harper Business.

[44] Aronson, E. (2011). *The social animal.* Worth Publishers.

[45] Pluckrose, H., & Lindsay, J. (2020). *Cynical theories: How activist scholarship made everything about race, gender, and identity—and why this harms everybody.* Pitchstone Publishing.

[46] Covey, S. R. (1989). *The 7 habits of highly effective people: Powerful lessons in personal change.* Free Press.

[47] Brown, B. (2010). *The gifts of imperfection: Let go of who you think you're supposed to be and embrace who you are.* Hazelden Publishing.

[48] Tutu, D., & Tutu, M. (2014). *The book of forgiving: The fourfold path for healing ourselves and our world.* HarperOne.

[49] Maxwell, J. C. (2012). *The 15 invaluable laws of growth: Live them and reach your potential.* Center Street.

[50] Cloud, H., & Townsend, J. (1992). *Boundaries: When to say yes, how to say no to take control of your life.* Zondervan.

[51] Brown, B. (2010). *The gifts of imperfection: Let go of who you think you're supposed to be and embrace who you are.* Hazelden Publishing.

[52] Neff, K. (2011). *Self-compassion: The proven power of being kind to yourself.* William Morrow.

[53] Stott, J. R. W. (2006). *The cross of Christ.* IVP Books.

[54] Wright, N. T. (2008). *Surprised by hope: Rethinking heaven, the resurrection, and the mission of the church.* HarperOne.

[55] Schwartz, S. H. (2012). An overview of the Schwartz theory of basic values. *Online Readings in Psychology and Culture, 2*(1). https://doi.org/10.9707/2307-0919.1116

[56] Lewis, C. S. (2001). *Mere Christianity*. HarperOne.

[57] EvanTell. (2020). Authenticity: The missing ingredient in evangelism today. *EvanTell*. https://evantell.org

[58] Pascal, B. (1995). *Pensées*. Penguin Classics.

[59] Willard, D. (1998). *The divine conspiracy: Rediscovering our hidden life in God*. HarperOne.

[60] Greene, J. (2013). *Moral tribes: Emotion, reason, and the gap between us and them*. Penguin Press.

[61] Smith, J. K. A. (2016). *You are what you love: The spiritual power of habit*. Brazos Press.

[62] Brown, B. (2010). *The gifts of imperfection: Let go of who you think you're supposed to be and embrace who you are*. Hazelden Publishing.

[63] Warren, R. (2002). *The purpose driven life: What on earth am I here for?* Zondervan.

[64] Foster, R. J. (1998). *Celebration of discipline: The path to spiritual growth*. HarperOne.

[65] Notholt, S. A. (2008). *Fields of fire: An atlas of ethnic conflict*. Stuart Notholt Communications.

[66] Bonhoeffer, D. (1995). *The cost of discipleship*. Touchstone.

[67] Krznaric, R. (2014). *Empathy: Why it matters, and how to get it*. TarcherPerigee.

[68] Bloom, P. (2016). *Against empathy: The case for rational compassion*. Ecco.

[69] Brown, B. (2012). *Daring greatly: How the courage to be vulnerable transforms the way we live, love, parent, and lead*. Gotham Books.

[70] Clear, J. (2018). *Atomic habits: An easy & proven way to build good habits & break bad ones*. Avery.

[71] Haidt, J. (2006). *The happiness hypothesis: Finding modern truth in ancient wisdom*. Basic Books.

[72] Nelson, K. (2012). *Ḥesed and the New Testament: An inter-textual categorization study*. Wipf and Stock Publishers.

[73] Keller, T. (2010). *Generous justice: How God's grace makes us just*. Penguin Books.

[74] Peterson, A. (2017). *Compassion and education: Cultivating compassionate children, schools, and communities*. Palgrave Macmillan.

[75] Fiensy, D. A. (2020). *Hear today: Compassion and grace in the parables of Jesus*. ACU Press & Leafwood Publishers.

[76] Brooks, D. (2015). *The road to character*. Random House.

[77] Maitland, M. (2012). *Pharaoh: King of Egypt*. British Museum Press.

[78] Boice, J. M. (2018). *The life of Moses: God's first deliverer of Israel.* Reformation Heritage Books.

[79] Gilbert, P. (2009). *The compassionate mind.* Constable & Robinson.

[80] Neff, K. (2011). *Self-compassion: The proven power of being kind to yourself.* William Morrow.

[81] Turkle, S. (2015). *Reclaiming conversation: The power of talk in a digital age.* Penguin Press.

[82] Kendall, R. T. (2007). *Total forgiveness: Revised and updated edition.* Charisma House.

[83] Singer, P. (2009). *The life you can save: How to do your part to end world poverty.* Random House.

[84] Siegel, D. J. (2007). *The mindful brain: Reflection and attunement in the cultivation of well-being.* W.W. Norton & Company.

[85] Dweck, C. S. (2006). *Mindset: The new psychology of success.* Random House.

[86] Taylor, C. (2007). *A secular age.* Belknap Press of Harvard University Press.

[87] Erickson, M. J. (2013). *Christian theology.* Baker Academic.

[88] Koenig, H. G. (2012). *Religion, spirituality, and health: The research and clinical implications. ISRN Psychiatry.* https://doi.org/10.5402/2012/278730

[89] Sternberg, R. J. (2003). *Wisdom, intelligence, and creativity synthesized*. Cambridge University Press.

[90] Cialdini, R. B. (2006). *Influence: The psychology of persuasion*. Harper Business.

[91] Brown, B. (2010). *The gifts of imperfection: Let go of who you think you're supposed to be and embrace who you are*. Hazelden Publishing.

[92] Goldstein, J. S. (2011). *Winning the war on war: The decline of armed conflict worldwide*. Dutton.

[93] Hanhimäki, J. M. (2015). *The United Nations: A very short introduction*. Oxford University Press.

[94] Harari, Y. N. (2018). *21 lessons for the 21st century*. Spiegel & Grau.

[95] Haidt, J. (2006). *The happiness hypothesis: Finding modern truth in ancient wisdom*. Basic Books.

[96] Bonhoeffer, D. (2015). *The cost of discipleship*. SCM Press.

[97] Sande, K. (2004). *The peacemaker: A biblical guide to resolving personal conflict*. Baker Books.

[98] Lewis, C. S. (2017). *The four loves*. HarperOne.

[99] Ken Sande, *The Peacemaker: A Biblical Guide to Resolving Personal Conflict* (Grand Rapids, MI: Baker Books, 2004), p. 45

[100] *Epoca*, III, nr. 353, January 17, 1897

[101] Arbinger Institute. (2006). *The anatomy of peace: Resolving the heart of conflict*. Berrett-Koehler Publishers.

[102] Nouwen, H. J. M. (1981). *The way of the heart: Connecting with God through prayer, wisdom, and silence*. Ballantine Books.

[103] Bonhoeffer, D. (1995). *The cost of discipleship*. Touchstone

[104] Tozer, A. W. (1982). *The pursuit of God*. Moody Publishers.

[105] Bonhoeffer, D. (1995). *The cost of discipleship*. Simon & Schuster.

[106] Lewis, C. S. (2001). *The problem of pain*. HarperOne.

[107] Ehrman, B. D. (2008). *God's problem: How the Bible fails to answer our most important question – Why we suffer*. HarperOne.

[108] Kinnaman, D., & Matlock, M. (2019). *Faith for exiles: 5 ways for a new generation to follow Jesus in digital Babylon*. Baker Books.

[109] Sun, K. (2021). 3 reasons that good intentions may lead to bad outcomes. *Psychology Today*.

[110] Longerich, P. (2015). *Goebbels: A biography*. Random House.

[111] Schafer, J. R. (August 2, 2018). The psychopathology of corruption. *Psychology Today*.

[112] Christakis, N. A., & Fowler, J. H. (2009). *Connected: The surprising power of our social networks and how they shape our lives*. Little, Brown and Company.

[113] Seligman, M. E. P. (2011). *Flourish: A visionary new understanding of happiness and well-being*. Atria Books.

[114] Wiking, M. (2017). *The little book of Lykke: Secrets of the world's happiest people*. Happiness Research Institute.

[115] Keltner, D. (2023). *Awe: The new science of everyday wonder and how it can transform your life*. Penguin Press.

[116] Cacioppo, J. T., & Patrick, W. (2008). *Loneliness: Human nature and the need for social connection*. W.W. Norton & Company.

[117] Holt-Lunstad, J., Smith, T. B., & Layton, J. B. (2015). Loneliness and social isolation as risk factors for mortality: A meta-analytic review. *American Psychologist, 70*(4), pp. 310–327.

https://doi.org/10.1037/a0039736

[18] Breggin, P. R. (2014). *Guilt, shame, and anxiety: Understanding and overcoming negative emotions*. Prometheus Books.

[119] Campbell, D. (2017). *Understanding your chronic dissatisfaction: A guide to emotional freedom and self-compassion*. CreateSpace Independent Publishing Platform.

[120] Rogers, C. R. (1995). *On becoming a person: A therapist's view of psychotherapy.* Houghton Mifflin Harcourt.

[121] Locke, E. A., & Latham, G. P. (2002). Building a practically useful theory of goal setting and task motivation: A 35-year odyssey. *American Psychologist, 57*(9), pp. 705-717. https://doi.org/10.1037/0003-066X.57.9.705

[122] Heiser, M. S. (2015). *The unseen realm: Recovering the supernatural worldview of the Bible.* Lexham Press.

[123] Dweck, C. S. (2007). *Mindset: The new psychology of success.* Ballantine Books.

[124] Kasser, T. (2002). *The high price of materialism.* MIT Press.

[125] Van Boven, L., & Gilovich, T. (2009). To do or to have? That is the question. *Journal of Consumer Research, 36*(1), pp. 14-27. https://doi.org/10.1086/597920

[126] Holt-Lunstad, J., Smith, T. B., Baker, M., Harris, T., & Stephenson, D. (2015). Loneliness and social isolation as risk factors for mortality: A meta-analytic review. *Perspectives on Psychological Science, 10*(2), 227-237. https://doi.org/10.1177/1745691614568352

[127] Seligman, M. E. P. (1993). *Learned helplessness: A theory for the age of personal control.* Oxford University Press.

[128] Foster, R. J. (2018). *Celebration of discipline: The path to spiritual growth.* HarperOne.

[129] Zimbardo, P. (2007). *The Lucifer Effect: Understanding How Good People Turn Evil*. Random House

[130] Festinger, L. (1957). *A Theory of Cognitive Dissonance*. Stanford University Press

Printed in Great Britain
by Amazon